TALKING FROM INFANCY

How to Nurture & Cultivate Early Language Development

by William Fowler

Center for Early Learning
and Child Care

Library of Congress Cataloging-in-Publication Data

Fowler, William, 1921-
    Talking from infancy : how to nurture and cultivate early language development / William Fowler.
        p.   cm.
    Includes bibliographical references.
    ISBN 0-914797-71-9
    1. Language acquisition—Parent participation.   I. Title.
P118.F65 1990
401'.93--dc20

          90-32791
          CIP

Book cover illustration by Auguste Renoir
Child with Toys — Gabrielle and the Artist's Son, Jean
Date: c. 1894, Oil on canvas
National Gallery of Art, Washington
Collection of Mr. and Mrs. Paul Mellon

Published by

Center for Early Learning and Child Care

29 Buckingham St., Cambridge, MA 02138
June 1995

Originally published by Brookline Books

Contents

Acknowledgments .... *iii*

Foreword *by Greta Fein* .... *v*

Preface .... *vii*

Chapter   *Page*

  1.   Questions About Language and Learning 1

  2.   Steps and Stages: Development and Experience 7

  3.   Sounds, Words, Sentences and Themes:
       Stages of Language Stimulation 15

  4.   How to Talk with Infants:
       Principles of Language Interaction 23

  5.   Where to Talk with Infants:
       Activities and Settings for Language Interaction 35

  6.   Stage I: Playing with Sounds (Vocalization Play) 71

  7.   Stage II: Playing with Words (Labeling Play) 77

  8.   Stage III: Playing with Phrases and Sentences 101

  9.   Stage IV: Theme Activities (Reading and Narrating) 119

10.   Starting Late: Correcting Language Delay 155

11.   Following the Infant's Progress 183

Appendix 219

References 227

Author's Biography 231

Index 233

ACKNOWLEDGEMENTS

Many teachers, parents, students and research colleagues, over the course of many projects in homes and day care, have contributed to the development of the ideas and methods presented in this book. To them all, I offer my deepest appreciation: To my students and research colleagues, especially Nasim Kahn, Karen Ogston, Gloria Roberts, Douglas Steane and Amy Swenson, for our most productive and enjoyable collaboration; to the staff and teachers of the Day Care Center of Canadian Mothercraft Society and of the Woodbine Day Care Center of Metro Toronto, along with the parents in all projects, for their untiring and creative efforts in developing and carrying out the programs with children; to our teachers, Dorothy Judd and Laurie Burgess, at the Center for Early Learning and Child Care, for their imaginative collaboration in putting the ideas on videotapes; and to Joe McVickers Hunt, one of the pioneers on early cognitive stimulation, for his ideas on vocalization play and his inspiration in recognizing the potentials of children for mental development.

Our studies in day care were made possible through the generous cooperation and support of the Board Directors of the Canadian Mothercraft Society and the Department of Social Services of Metropolitan Toronto. We are also indebted to research grants from the Atchinson Charitable Foundation and the Ontario Institute for Studies in Education for our studies at the Canadian Mothercraft Day Care Centre; and to research grants from the Canada Department of National Health and Welfare and the Research Planning Branch of the Ontario Ministry of Community and Social Services, who together commissioned and funded the research at the Woodbine Day Care Centre.

I would also like to add a note of thanks to my daughter, Josephine, whose editing helped to clarify ideas and improve the readability of the manuscript. And above all I would like to thank the children, including my own three daughters, Velia Mauri, Monique and Josephine, who shared their infancy with us in ways I hope gave as much meaning and joy to their lives as the experiences did for me and my colleagues.

Foreword

In this volume, William Fowler brings together two decades of work with the parents and teachers of young children. The setting for the book is Dr. Fowler's conclusion that the educational focus likely to be most beneficial for infants, toddlers, and preschoolers is one that stresses language enrichment. Children who receive early language enrichment not only become more proficient in language, but are more competent in other areas as well. This conclusion is consistent with results of the New Haven Parent Early Education study which compared the effects of three curricular concentrations (language, social interaction, play) on children's development during the second and third years of life. The language curriculum was the most effective of the three.

Why are the language enrichment activities described in this book so effective? The answer may lie in an area that early educators and developmental psychologists have neglected. We know quite a bit about early development and the interactive conditions that optimize this development. But we know relatively little about the adult who participates in these interactions. Often, we view this adult as infinitely malleable. We assume that with sound information and some demonstration the adult will replace inadequate interactions with optimal ones. But it may be easier to change adult behavior in some areas than in others. Language might be easier for three reasons.

First, adults will do best by talking to children about things that they value. Most adults agree that speaking and communicating is an important area of learning. By comparison, stacking three blocks or playing house may seem like a childish activity of little intrinsic value. Language is a more tangible performance than thinking or problem solving. It is easier to identify a sound, word, or sentence than to see the thought that goes into building a tower. Parents and teachers may be more likely to do what the experts recommend if they believe in its aims and if they can readily recognize points of entry.

Second, adults will do best with children by using those things for which the adults themselves have acquired competence. Language is an area of high proficiency even for those adults who are not especially fluent as measured on standardized tests. We ask them to monitor the child's competence and to choose things to say that fit the context and the child's level of understanding. Adults, even those without formal training, know how to choose words and phrases and how to use intuitive strategies for monitoring their own comprehension and that of others. So when we train parents and teachers to use enriched ways of talking with children, we build on well-established adult strengths and competencies.

Third, and perhaps most important, a program of language enrichment might provide a pleasant path to enriched social interaction between adult and child. What might matter most is the increase in affect, interest, expressiveness, and responsiveness that accompany the language enrichment activities described in this book.

Some readers might study the text, others might prefer the boxes, and some might do both. Some might scrupulously follow the program that Dr. Fowler maps out, and others might choose a bit here and a bit there. Whatever the reader's aim and persistence, this volume has much to offer those who rear and care for the young.

GRETA FEIN

Professor of Psychology and Early Childhood Education
Director, Center for Young Children
University of Maryland
College Park, Maryland

Rearing Children in Contemporary Society

Our contemporary world faces three major problems in rearing children: (1) the increasing fragmentation of community and family life; (2) a serious shortage of quality child care; and (3) the multiplying demands for socializing children in the complex symbol and thinking skills increasingly demanded by our high tech society. The common family of today consists of working parents or too often the single parent, typically commuting long distances and living isolated from the traditional supports of the extended family and local community. Long hours and isolation makes day care essential to furnish the care and intellectual stimulation that parents are no longer able to provide for much of every child's day. Yet, because of the widespread shortage of professional care systems, parents are often forced to rely on the substitute care of untrained home care providers. Group day care itself, when available, is frequently hampered by limited resources.

Child Rearing in Earlier Times

It was not always like this. The traditional setting for family life and child rearing for millennia has been the small, tightly knit rural community. Children grew up learning the skills of adult life through observing and imitating the activities of older children and adults who were readily visible in their daily life. Home and work were always close together and little formal tutelage was necessary for them to acquire competence in the informal language and concrete, hand tool agricultural or hunting and domestic skills required to cope in the local subsistence economies.

The first real changes began with the industrial age, beginning in the sixteenth century, which brought many disruptions to family and community as mothers and children were recruited to labor long hours in appalling conditions and live in densely crowded, filthy urban slums. Widespread reforms over the course of the 19th century led to the abolition of child labor, the improvement in working conditions through the efforts of labor unions, and the establishment of universal public education. While substantial numbers of women continued to work, most deferred entry to the working world of formal jobs until the child entered school at age 5 or 6. With mothers caring for children during their early years in family life still centered in the local community, more or less until after World War II, the traditional forms of child care were adequate in preparing children for school and the varied opportunities of the workaday world.

Competence Goals for Children in the Modern World

The advent of the computer-driven, high tech society of recent decades, however, has scaled competence demands upward for everyone at a time when the further breakup of family and community undermines whatever effectiveness the traditional patterns of informal home-based early education had in preparing young children for school and adult life. The magnitude of the dilemma between the heightened demands for competence in contemporary society and how modes of child rearing and the schools are failing to socialize children and develop competence is underlined by a recent editorial in *Science*, the journal of the American Association for the Advancement of Science: our country increasingly faces "the prospect of millions of youngsters entering the work force without basic language and math skills" (Grogan, 1990). Clearly, special efforts are needed to buttress the quality of early home care and extend the availability of quality day care to prepare children for school and a world of work based on manipulating verbal and mathematical symbols in increasingly abstract and intricate ways.

 The problem is more than one of ensuring plenty of love and attention to the care of infants and young children. The informal communication skills built into the traditional forms of child rearing, even when well grounded in tender loving care, do not take account of the quality and abstractions of language and thought needed for today's world. Early experience exercises a profound influence on development. It is during infancy and early childhood that the foundation for the child's understanding and modes of coping with the world are established. A firm cognitive system is as important as a strong and secure emotional foundation. What the child begins with is what the child must build upon during later opportunities for learning. A poor foundation makes it difficult for children to master what is culturally expected in the next stage, while a strong foundation enables children to assimilate successive demands very easily and even go beyond the average range of these demands and learn on their own.

The Importance of Language

Language plays a central role in the process of developing competence in the modern world. The foundation that children need in infancy today pivots on verbal skills. The era of informal communication and direct action skills so prominent in the past has been replaced by an era that is built on manipulating language in highly abstract and varied forms that make use of the endless variety of complex ideas that are generated almost daily. Communication can no longer be confined to using familiar expressions with familiar people who share common local concerns. Constantly appearing new and complex ideas, unrelated to shared communities and personal backgrounds, require the ability to use language in highly general and abstract ways to explore matters totally out of context of common personal experiences.

My Research on Early Language Stimulation

Just how important language developed in this way is to the development of intellectual competence in children became increasingly clear in the course of my research on early language stimulation. This research began in earnest with two studies in day care. Years earlier I had carried out a great deal of verbal stimulation with my three infant daughters, but this effort, much like my other research for some years, largely consisted of general programs of early intellectual development and did not pay special attention to how children's language skills developed.

The results of my research on early language stimulation are summarized in detail in an appendix at the end of this book. Briefly, what the studies demonstrate is how easy it is to stimulate children's language development. They also show that nearly all children, regardless of the family's social and educational background, can benefit from special attention to language, beginning in earliest infancy. Nearly all of the children in the research groups developed language skills better and at faster rates than the norms for their cultural and educational background. They began to understand and say words earlier, and to form phrases and sentences better. Further, all 13 of the children followed into adolescence excelled in school, especially in verbal skills.

Implications of Our Research Findings

It would appear that our fragmented communities and family life have failed to adapt methods of child care and stimulation needed for the highly verbal, abstract symbol-oriented modes characteristic of contemporary institutions. Just as important, current common modes of child rearing fail to help children attain their full mental potentials. These statements are amply supported by the following conclusions that emerged from our research:

- *An early start with an enriched environment generally has very significant positive influences on cognitive development.*

- *When early enrichment is centered on language experiences, it has the strongest effects on children's verbal development.*

- *Early language stimulation also seems to exercise a strong general influence on mental and social development.* This general advantage shows up in problem solving, but to some extent in all skills, including social competence, and is reflected in children's elevated IQ scores and excellent performance in school, all of which are based heavily on verbal skills but include general concepts and reasoning as well.

  Especially heartening is the influence early verbal competence has upon children's social development and motivation. These advancing verbal concept skills give infants the tools to understand and communicate with adults and their peers, enabling them to interact more rationally, to participate in and initiate their own projects and learning activities, to take care of their own needs sooner, to follow directions, and get along more independently and comfortably.

  While this generalized development may be in part attributable to the emphasis placed on concept understanding in our approach to language stimulation, it would also seem to be inherent in the power of language to represent complex ideas and help in coping with the world around us.

- *Also exciting is the potential of early language gains from enrichment to continue through later periods of development.* They do not maintain themselves without continued attention and support, however. While enriching language during infancy also helps infants to become self-directed in pursuing ideas and learning on their own, only children whose families continue to provide reasonably rich environments and emotional support will continue to develop and achieve at high levels in school. Early experience is invaluable in establishing a strong and complex foundation of language and other mental skills and interest in learning, but continuing enrichment also appears to be essential.

- *The effects of enriching language during infancy appear to be equally effective in both home and day care settings.* The problem is not the setting or who the caregivers are, it is the quality of caring and attention supplied and the fact that the quality must be continued throughout the child's development in all settings in which the child is cared for, at least over the preschool and early school years. In our studies, children continued to advance at high levels as long as the quality of enriched care was maintained in both the home and day care; when care quality declined, so did the children's rate of language development.

- *Early enrichment is potentially equally effective with infants from all social, educational and linguistic backgrounds, when families are furnished with adequate and continuing educational guidance and social support.* Because of having fewer resources, however, continuing support from professionals, either through home guidance or access to quality day care, becomes more critical with socioeconomically disadvantaged families than with advantaged families who possess the resources to continue the enrichment on their own.

- *Contrary to expectations, infants from multi-sibling families (averaging close to 2 per family in the day care studies and including 6 second or third born infants among the home reared) appear to develop as well as single, first born infants.* In some cases attention may have been slightly diluted, especially when siblings were closely spaced, but since 3 multi-sibling home reared infants (2 of them second born) were among the most advanced and fluent infants, the increased demands for rearing 2 or more (3 with 2 siblings) children do not seem to be insurmountable obstacles to enriching the infant's language environment.

- *The maintenance of quality care with enriched language need not be an elaborate enterprise.* It does not require much extra effort or even ideal child care ratios to provide stimulating language experiences for children. It is largely a matter of becoming aware of the value of interacting with children in certain easy to learn ways and realizing that how you interact with them will make an enormous difference in how well they develop.

Our research studies are not the only ones that demonstrate the value of early enriched experience. The Civil Rights Movement of the 1960's and 1970's inspired a tremendous amount of research effort with infants and preschool children, devoted especially to improving the early environment of children from poor socioeconomic circumstances and diverse ethnic backgrounds (Consortium for Longitudinal Studies, 1983; Fowler, 1983; Zigler & Valentine, 1979).

When better experimental programs were developed, especially those with concentrated emphasis on language, and when the programs were continued for some years, the children's development advanced correspondingly, much beyond that of the cultural norms for their peers (Consortium, 1983; Garber & Heber, 1981; Hunt, 1986). The advanced development continued, moreover, as long as the enrichment and support of some sort was maintained. In one study, for example, infants reared in an orphanage for poor and abandoned infants, employing a specially enriched child care and language stimulation program, made outstanding language and cognitive gains that were later maintained because the infants were adopted into stable, adequate families (Hunt, 1986).

Thus the setting and family background matter less than the quality of care. Enriching the lives of our infants is essential for them to start life with a strong foundation to attain their full potential for development. Following up with the same kind of care at all age levels is equally necessary for the child to develop to his or her full potential.

The Problem of Expectations

This book has been written to help caregivers, parents, day care teachers, nannies, and other practitioners to understand ways to enrich the language experience of young children. One of the biggest obstacles to establishing enriched care for infants our staff repeatedly encountered was the low expectations both day care teachers and parents initially had for infant language development. I remember so often hearing teachers comment in response to our efforts to encourage them to talk regularly with the young babies as they cared for and played with them, saying "But they won't understand, they can't talk yet." This was especially true in the day care setting, where teachers had a pre-learned skepticism that was a result of their prior training. It was less true of student teachers in a private agency and of first-time parents, because their expectations were less formed. We overcame this caution by patiently and persistently asking parents and teachers to try the procedures and see what happened.

In the end, what always convinced caregivers was to see the effects on the infants after a few weeks of using language generously in daily care. In the day care settings, teachers would gradually see how well the infants progressed in responding vocally, and beginning to understand and say words with attention and interest. When they began to compare the development of these infants with those who had already been attending day care for some months without the enriched language stimulation, they became enthusiastic about the whole idea, sometimes quite suddenly. From then on, they talked quite regularly and with interest to all the babies, even the youngest.

In the home, parents would start to become convinced and enthusiastic about the process as they saw how quickly and well their infant started to understand the words they used regularly. Perhaps the most convincing evidence for parents appeared when they got together with friends with infants of similar age, or even older, seeing how well their infant was doing compared to the other infants.

Who the Book is For

The guidelines discussed in this book are written for caregivers in all settings. They are designed to foster the development of infants to reach their full potentials of language competence, a goal to which all children are entitled but which many children never have the opportunity to realize.

This book is not a panacea. It is intended to make a small contribution toward the effort to expand the quality of infant care. There is no book quite like it available. It is not, unlike most books on language learning, designed only for remedial work with language-delayed children, although it may be useful with such children as well (See Chapter 10). It is a book for all caregivers in all settings, in the home and day care, on useful principles for enriching the language experiences of infants from all backgrounds.

I have tried to minimize the use of jargon, in particular to avoid discussing language processes with linguistic terms that might impede understanding. I have also attempted to bridge the worlds of home and day care, for the most part discussing methods and conditions in ways that apply equally to all settings, but addressing concerns for the different settings where appropriate.

To complement this book, there will soon be available a set of videotapes illustrating these same principles and activities of language interaction at four major stages of language development, following much the same approach discussed in this book. The tapes show scenes of parents, teachers, and myself interacting in play activities and child care routines with infants and young children from a few months to three years of age. Information on where the tapes may be obtained is available from the Center for Early Learning and Child Care, Inc., 29 Buckingham St, Cambridge, MA 02138.

How the Book Is to Be Used

The book presents a comprehensive picture of methods and conditions for enriching children's language experiences, from earliest infancy through the preschool years. The first two chapters cover general questions about language and learning (Chapter 1) and the course of development and the role of experience (Chapter 2). The next three chapters outline the stages of interaction for enhancing language development (Chapter 3), principles and procedures to be used (Chapter 4), and the many settings and activities in which to interact for fostering development (Chapter 5). The next four chapters review the methods to be employed in detail for each of the four stages of development. How to play with sounds (vocalization play) beginning from earliest infancy is discussed in Chapter 6; playing with words is covered in Chapter 7; the expansion of language play into learning how to use different parts of speech and form phrases and sentences is discussed in Chapter 8; and learning how to use language fluently in extended discourse, such as conversations, discussions and relating experiences is discussed at length in Chapter 9. The final two chapters outline procedures to be used in working with moderately language-delayed infants (Chapter 10) and methods of evaluating the child's development, ranging from formal ways of testing to practical ways of charting an infant's progress from day to day (Chapter 11).

It is important to emphasize the value of flexibility of these distinctions. You must adapt to each child's individual level and style of functioning. The aim is not to pressure, but to work with the child in play and easy styles of care, and to show the child examples of language that they are ready to learn at their own pace.

How to Get Started

Some parents and day care teachers may at first feel lost at where to start. There is no simple, magic formula, but it is not difficult at all to get started. Whether you are a parent or teacher in day care, the procedures are much the same. For the youngest infants under 3 or 4 months, it takes little more than establishing face to face contact in talking and listening to their vocal efforts. For older infants, just begin by sitting down with the child and informally talking about the objects and actions you both use in play. Adapt how you proceed according to the child's stage of language development and follow the principles suggested in Chapters 4 and 5.

For older infants who are behind in development, start in the same way, by engaging the infant in play and adapting your language play to the child's specific problem areas. Regardless of the child's age and individual differences, most caregivers will find little difficulty in successfully following through with the guidelines in this book.

It is hoped that parents and day care teachers from diverse circumstances can make use of the guidelines in this book. I believe that most infants can be helped to develop in ways that are more interesting, exciting, and verbally and socially competent, adding to the ease and joys of all of us in rearing children at home or in day care. Good luck.

Figure 1-1. One of My Research Children at 10 months

Chapter 1

Questions About Language and Learning

THE EARLY HISTORY OF BILLY*

By the time Billy was 15 months old he could combine words regularly to make two-word phrases like, "Daddy's cup," "out go," and "up please," and was beginning to construct three-word sentences, such as "I want that" and "I want two." He also had a vocabulary of more than 50 words. Most children can't say two-word phrases until at least 20 months, know 50 words until 21 months, and they don't usually make any three-word sentences until 23 months or more.

By 22 months Billy could make his wants known quite easily in sentences of 4 or 5 words, and sometimes more. What pleased his parents most was the way he understood things, could follow directions, and figure things out. "He's way ahead of where his sister (now 4 1/2) was at the same age. He's so reasonable and catches on so easily," Billy's mother commented. "My friends notice this, their babies can say no more than a few words and don't seem to understand much, and wonder why he's so advanced. Billy prefers to play with his sister or the older kids at the playground, when they will let him."

How did Billy get so advanced? Many people would say it is just because he is a bright boy, adding, if they think about it, that he was just born that way or has superior genes. Perhaps they are partly right, but in

---

* Billy is a pseudonym (to preserve his privacy) for one of the children in our series of research studies.

this case at least there is more to it than that. Billy is one of the many children whose parents (or teachers in the day care projects) participated in one of my research projects on enriching a baby's language environment from the early months of life. Teachers in day care and parents in the home were specially tutored by our research staff who showed them how to pay more attention to language learning than most caregivers do, especially in the important early period. The idea is to embed lots of talk with infants in their daily activities, informally and in play, as a matter of routine.

THE IMPORTANCE OF EXPERIENCE

Is all this extra attention really necessary? Does it really make that much difference, especially with a bright child like Billy? Actually, whether a child is born basically "smart" or "just average," these are only biological *potentials* for ability that must be developed. However important biology is, abilities are useless without an environment that fosters their development. Unlike dogs and cats and other animals, whose abilities can't go far even with life-long training, human beings require years of intensive care and mental stimulation for their abilities to reach their full potential. The brains of newborn babies are relatively so much less developed, yet potentially so much more complex than those of any other animal. Whatever a child's inherited potential, a long process of development through experience is essential for children to fulfill that potential.

But don't most parents and teachers talk a lot to their babies anyway, except for infants reared in broken homes or families in very stressful circumstances? Don't most children come out all right, except in problem families, with of course some children becoming smarter or better at language because they have better genes?

Actually parents and teachers differ a great deal in how well and frequently they talk to babies, and perhaps surprisingly, this is even true among well-educated parents. The issue, moreover, is not just how *much* parents and other caregivers talk to babies, although this is important. It is the *way* in which they use language in caring for infants. Many caregivers talk a great deal but too rapidly or not focused in a way that helps the infant to learn. It means becoming aware that what you say and how you say it makes a difference in how easily and well the infant learns to talk.

While *both* the quality and quantity of adult speech directly addressed to the baby are important, this does not really mean spending a lot of extra time. It only means accompanying the many hours of routine care babies need with individualized talk, plus spending a few brief periods each day in special language play with toys and books. Few parents or day caregivers can't improve the ways in which they help a baby's language grow.

But is it so important that Billy was way ahead of most other children as a baby? Won't the others catch up, at least the smart ones, once they begin the give and take of conversation with other children and adults, especially during the school years? While that seems reasonable, an early start leads to more and more proficiency as the child develops, mostly because fluent toddlers can relate more easily to older children and adults who teach them more advanced concepts because they can understand more. Early competence leads to cumulatively greater skill as development progresses. Time that might otherwise be spent in learning the ordinary things or in catching up can be spent in learning more and more difficult things, leading the average and delayed child to fall further and further behind.

THE CENTRAL ROLE OF LANGUAGE

Why focus on language? Aren't other abilities, like knowledge and social skills, just as important? What is language anyway? We pay so much attention to language because it seems to be at the root of so many other skills, including our knowledge and how well we get along socially. Children learn about the world in large part through parents and teachers explaining things or reading about things, processes which are both rooted heavily in language. It is true that children also learn through doing things on their own and by pictures, but without explanations and comments to guide them they don't learn nearly as well or as easily. They also learn from television and movies, but here again language carries much of the weight of the ideas.

Language is so key because it enables us to talk about the world and represent things in abstract terms. Once children have mastered this abstract code, they don't need to actually touch or see things in order to talk about them to others and even discuss how things might be different. And of course language is so flexible that totally new ideas, as in stories, inventions, and religious concepts, can be put into words, explained in detail and changed around in any combination, just by manipulating speech. Thus language is an extraordinarily powerful and flexible tool for thinking and planning before we act and for communicating to other

---

Box 1
The Nature of Language

What Language Is:

An abstract code for representing and communicating ideas about the world through speech and writing.

Uses of Language:

1) Represent concepts about the world in shorthand form.

2) Enable people to communicate complex and abstract ideas.

3) Express feelings in meaningful, intricate, and varied ways.

4) Together these uses make possible the development of people as social beings, living and working in extremely complex societies with endlessly varying relations, institutions, and forms of communication.

Forms of Language:

1) Speech: Many thousands of different spoken languages and dialects have evolved in the course of human existence through the varying experiences of different cultures and subcultures, though not all are still used.

2) Writing: Virtually all of the world's currently spoken languages and many of those no longer spoken have been represented in written codes.

---

people ideas about real or imagined things. Without language, our complex social world of work and play could not even be imagined, let alone developed, and human history would remain unremembered, untold in stories, and by extension in its written form, unrecorded through books.

Skill in language is the major component of most IQ tests and of successful learning in school. Think about what the child learns in school most of the day through teacher instruction, recitation and exchanging ideas with other children (through language), and reading primers and workbooks, and later texts and tests in all the various subjects (using language in its written form). Arithmetic and other forms of mathematics are also complex variations and extensions of the language code, and of course different languages are simply different forms of basic language coding. It is difficult to overestimate the value of language for schooling, human development and society.

Figure 2-1. Language Enrichment Play

Chapter 2

Steps and Stages: Development and Experience

THE COURSE OF LANGUAGE DEVELOPMENT

Children learn to talk over a series of steps and stages. First they utter miscellaneous sounds. These are loosely formed versions of various sounds human beings are biologically capable of making with their voice box (larynx), tongue, and mouth movements. These more or less resemble some of the vowels and consonants found in various languages. Then they begin to repeat particular sounds that are closer to ones their family and others use in the local language. Next they begin to combine these sounds into pairs and then strings, babbling in sometimes long chains of language-sounding patterns.

The first distinguishable words are soon heard, but they are first used only as names or designations for particular persons or pets. These typically include the words for father and mother (in English, "da-da" and "ma-ma") and perhaps the name of the family pet or a cherished, cuddly toy. Not long after, the first two or three real words appear. These are usually names for familiar objects, such as ball, dog, and cookie, which begin to be recognized as generalized labels that can be applied to more than just the child's own ball, dog, or cookie. Gradually more and more words come into the infant's repertoire, until new words appear at a rate almost too fast to keep track of. At the same time the infant learns to use them more and more widely but with increasing accuracy with the right objects.

About the time infants have packed away about 20 or so words into their vocabulary, parents often suddenly hear them create two-word phrases fraught with personal meaning, like "baby up," "daddy shoe," or "want ball." Word combinations may then multiply more or less rapidly, as the child moves into multi-word phrases and complete sentences with extended syntax almost without notice. At this point, the beginnings of full speech have arrived. Later development involves gradually stringing sentences together in extended conversation and narrative speech organized around themes, and then gradually in increasingly abstract forms.

Order and Experience

The foregoing sequence is a path all children travel to acquire the basic beginnings of language, but they follow it at different rates and with certain other important variations according to their environment. They follow a general sequence of learning sounds first, followed by words, sentences and narrative speech, the order for which is determined by how language is put together. They also generally learn the different parts of speech in order of their difficulty, easier words like the names of concrete things (doll, car) and frequent action terms (up, down, sit) and expressions (bye-bye) usually preceding the more complex terms like adjectives and pronouns, simply because they are easier to learn.

Yet while these stages of development are universal, children vary widely in the *rate* at which they progress and the extent to which they master each stage. These varied rates of language learning are determined by the quality and type of their language experiences. For the same reasons they also vary considerably in which words in any category they learn first (e.g., milk, cookie or car), and to some degree in the order in which they learn the different parts of speech. For example, the child's first words may include an adjective or two (e.g., more, big) and even occasionally a pronoun like "that," though the easier object names invariably predominate. And children will also vary enormously in how *well* they master the complexities of language in all its forms. Not all children reach the same levels of competence. In fact, research studies of Carew (1980), Clarke-Stewart (1973), Huttenlocher et al. (1991), McCartney (1984), and myself (Fowler, 1983) have shown that most of the variation in children's language and intellectual competencies are produced through differences in their early language experiences with adults. The most pronounced differences in competence are not simply in vocabulary size and richness of expression, but also in the ability to discuss abstract themes that are out of the context of familiar times and places.

Thus experience can make a great deal of difference. How clearly children speak, how fast they learn and, more important, how well they learn all the intricacies will depend on the quality of their language environment from day to day over the first few years of development. All infants born without birth injuries and without defects in their nervous system are capable of learning language, and most children are capable of learning language fluently and skillfully in complicated ways. Yet it is probably safe to say that only a few children really grow up with the kind of language experiences that develop their skills to their full potential.

THE EFFECT OF ENRICHMENT ON DEVELOPMENT

Just how much difference does a high quality of language experience make in how well infants learn to talk? One answer to this question is shown in the accompanying Box 2, which compares the rates of language development for children who enjoyed a greatly enriched language environment from early infancy with the average rates for children who experience the usual amounts of attention to language.

The figures for the enriched column are taken from a series of research studies (in both the home and day care settings) that my students and I conducted on the effects of early language stimulation on development, which followed the same methods Billy's parents used, as described in Chapter 1. The families came from widely varying walks of life, educational levels, and ethnic backgrounds. These ranged from unskilled trades to the professions, from grade school to graduate degrees, and included Chinese and Italian-speaking families. In general, boys and girls progressed about equally well, as did the infants from both poorly and highly educated families. As Box 2 shows, both the average and enriched infants follow the same general sequence in language development, but at very different rates.

Later Development

As development progresses, children continue to vary more widely in the quality and range of their competencies in using language. Past the preschool years, at later stages, there are many refinements and complexities in language on which children's rates of learning differ enormously. Keeping antecedents straight, distinguishing active and passive voice, using the right object pronoun, organizing compound sentences with

Box 2
The Course of Early Language Development:
Age Norms for Language Achievement for Infants from Average and Enriched Language Environments

		Age Ranges of Acquisition (Months)	
Stages	*Steps*	*Average Environment[a]*	*Enriched Environment[b]*
Sounds (Vocalization)			
	Miscellaneous sounds	0-1	
	Vowels and Consonants	1-5	
	2 syllable repetitions	6-7	5-6
	Babbled strings	7-8	6-7
Words			
	Understanding (recognizes name of some objects)	8-9	6-8
	Says ma-ma, da-da (and other names)	9-10	7-8
	Imitates words	10-11	7-9
	First real words (3)	11-12	7-9
	10-20 word vocabulary	18-20	9-11
Phrases & Sentences			
	Imitates 2 to 3 word combinations	18-20	11-12
	Two-word combinations	20-22	12-13
	Three-word phrase-sentences	22-24	13-16
	Talks in sentences	24-27	16-24
Themes (Connected speech)			
	Relates experiences	33-36	21-24
	Uses basic rules of grammar	48	24+

[a] Taken from various mental scales and research measures, including the REEL Scale, Griffiths Scales (1954; 1970) and Menyuk (1977).

[b] Project measurement began only at 4 to 5 months.

logically clear relations between independent and dependent clauses, and other complex rules of grammar are not watched closely in colloquial speech. Such rules are generally reserved for the formal logical expression and niceties of school learning and business and academic environments.

Language development in the later stages also moves in widely different directions as a result of children developing widely diverging interests, such as acquiring different languages and eventually developing more distinctive writing styles associated with various fields. Sports and computers, stamp collecting and history, carpenter and clerical work, are all worlds with specialized vocabularies and communication patterns. Some languages may be constructed of somewhat more complex rules than others, such as Chinese compared to Spanish, but most differences in complexity are the result of differences in skill and background that influence competence in second language learning. Adults in particular must make conscious efforts to learn and adapt to sounds and rules quite different from those they have come to know so well. Newspaper journalists, historians, scientists, poets, and fiction writers develop markedly different modes of speaking and writing. In general there is an accumulating diversity of language skills with age, tied to differences in interest and style as well as further development in competence levels. Different courses of development will build in different directions out of later experiences.

Because the focus of this book is on the early years, these later developmental learning tasks need not concern us. It is useful to note however, that children who learn to speak fluently during the early years are likely to encounter little difficulty in mastering the mysteries of these later complexities, whatever later route they elect to follow. Our own research studies illustrate this very well. In our follow-up studies into high school/college of the children who experienced enriched language stimulation during infancy, nearly all of them have been outstanding students in school (See Appendix for details). Their exceptional competencies have been concentrated in language, reading and other verbally related skills, including creative story writing, foreign language learning and math, but many are also skilled in science and one or more forms of art. Quite a number have mastered more than one foreign language and their social competence has been generally well rounded, including a wide range of interests and active pursuit of extra curricular activities. Nearly all students were very much self-directed in learning and achievement.

Thus the quality of the foundation the child acquires in the early years has endless implications for the possibilities of diversification of language and thought in later development. While a firm mastery of language during infancy is no guarantee of later skill or elegance of style, it is never easy to build on a shaky foundation. I now turn to the program of early language stimulation used so successfully in our collected studies.

Figure 3-4. *Stage IV: Theme Activity*

PHOTO BY SARAH PUTNAM

Figure 3-3. *Stage III:*
Sentence Play

VIDEO PHOTO BY MICHAEL MAJOROS

Figure 3-2. *Stage II: Word Play*

PHOTO BY CATHY HOLAHAN

Figure 3-1. *Stage I: Vocalization Play*

PHOTO BY SARAH PUTNAM

Stages of Language Interaction

Chapter 3

Sounds, Words, Sentences and Themes

STAGES OF LANGUAGE STIMULATION

The methods used so successfully in our research consist of a number of comparatively simple principles for parents, teachers, and other caregivers to use daily with their infants in a variety of different activities and situations. They may be used with equal effectiveness in the home and day care and by any type of caregiver, parents and professionals alike, whether they be adults or older siblings. One may start with infants at any age, though the earlier one starts and the more regularly and sensitively the methods are applied, the more effective the results.

Because these methods always bring into focus relations between words and what they represent through social interaction between caregiver and child, the approach integrates the referential or representational basis of language with its social and communicative functions. At the same time, as development occurs, the ordinary conversations of everyday activity provide more extended experience in the social functions of language.

In this chapter I will briefly outline the stages and steps in stimulating development, which of course follow the logic of the natural order of development outlined in the previous chapter. In Chapter 4, I will discuss the principles we have used in our research for how to interact to enrich language development. This discussion will be followed in Chapter 5 by a discussion on how the principles can be applied to different activities. Detailed discussion of the practices followed at each of the four stages will be taken up in Chapters 6 through 9. The primary framework is always one of establishing a good foundation for language during early childhood, though I will also touch on the child's mastery of language for literary, academic and scientific purposes during later periods of development.

STAGES OF LANGUAGE LEARNING

The processes for helping infants learn language are organized into a chart presented in Box 3, and outlined in more detail in Box 4 below, following the four stages outlined in Box 2.

Each stage corresponds to a basic dimension or building block of language, at successive levels of the organization of language: sound patterns form words, words combine to make phrases and sentences, and finally sentences are combined to make up strings of connected ideas (themes). The stages of interaction naturally follow the normal order of development that all infants have to go through to learn to talk. They can't learn words before they master a few sounds, sentences before they know a few words (around 20), or present ideas in connected speech before they have mastered a few sentences.

Starting ages are approximate, since infants should always be stimulated in language according to their readiness for advancement, not simply according to age. Progress depends more on experience than on age. Our research has shown that infants are ready for sound play in the earliest months, and that word play can profitably begin as early as three or four months of age, leading infants to begin understanding words by 6 to 8 months and say their first real words by 7 to 9 months, sometimes earlier. These starting ages are obviously well ahead of achievement norms, which reflect the experiences of average children in unenriched environments. But in fact they are also ahead of the achievement bench-

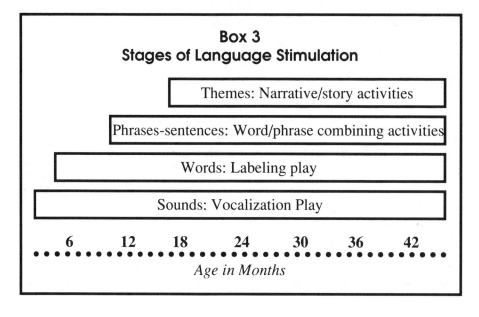

Box 3
Stages of Language Stimulation

Themes: Narrative/story activities

Phrases-sentences: Word/phrase combining activities

Words: Labeling play

Sounds: Vocalization Play

6   12   18   24   30   36   42

Age in Months

marks for children exposed to enriched language environments (Box 2). Clearly, waiting until they reach a norm would mean delaying development until after the norm. The ages indicated in Boxes 3 and 4 for the later stages of sentence learning and theme activities are also based on our research observations of infant readiness for advancement, assuming an enriched start with sound and word learning.

It will be noted from Box 3 that there is considerable overlap among the stages during later phases. Infants do not progress through the stages along a rigid pathway. Babies sometimes make mental leaps on their own and will usually catch on better if a somewhat flexible course is adopted by the caregiver, one which moves back and forth between adjacent steps more or less within the same level. Although understanding and speech follow a certain order, infants are also likely to move back and forth among the stages, in part because each stage involves increasingly complex concepts that only become mastered when the infant begins to learn the rules of later stages. For example, infants will begin to learn words before they know all sounds, and start to combine words into simple phrases before they know many words.

More complex parts of speech such as adjectives, adverbs, pronouns and conjunctions must be worked within sentences to be fully grasped. Even when children begin to make streams of sentences to develop conversational themes, they still need experience in learning syntax and grammar and to expand their vocabulary development. Infants will also pick up concepts about different stages from the ordinary conversations of daily life and occasional unintended examples you use with them in play. Still, it helps to stick somewhat closely to the child's stage, especially during the early stages; gradually moving to the next stage in order to make it easier for them to master concepts along the way will be most productive.

STARTING LATE

Although starting special language stimulation early has shown obvious developmental advantages in our studies, all is not lost if an infant is well along in age before starting a special program of enrichment. Beginning to concentrate on language activities at later ages, even if an infant has been talked with very little before 6, 12, or even 18 months of age will do much to establish competent speech, certainly better than if the child were to continue developing in a relatively barren language environment. Chances are the infant has already learned something about language

Box 4
Language Stimulation at
Successive Stages of Development

Stage	Learning Activities	Approximate Starting Ages(a) (months)

I. Sounds: Vocalization Play   Birth on

Talk with infant in face-to-face contact.
Imitate the infant's "speech" sounds.
Make new sounds for infant to imitate.
Interact to get a "dialogue" going.
Order for introducing new sounds:
   A. single vowels and consonants
   B. repetitive syllables (ba-ba, ga-ga)
   C. syllable combinations (ba-da, ka-gi)

II. Words: Labeling Play   3 or over

Name things the infant spontaneously looks at and/or touches.
Draw the infant's attention to and name things.
Order in which to introduce parts of speech:
   A. **Simple Parts of Speech:**
        1) small, familiar objects (nouns): hand, cup
        2) concrete actions (verbs): touch, kiss; "up"
   B. **Complex Parts of Speech:**
        1) prepositions: in, out, on, off
        2) adjectives: big, little; this, that
        3) adverbs: fast, slowly; here, there
        4) conjunctions: and, or, but
        5) articles: a, an; the
        6) pronouns: I, you, me, it, we; this, that

General Activities: use greetings, expressions and simple
   instructions in ordinary communications; begin picture books.

Box 4 (cont.)

Stage	Learning Activities	Approximate Starting Ages[a] (months)

III. Phrases-Sentences: Sentence Play   9 or over

Combine words into phrases: **daddy + go** and phrases
   into sentences: **Mary runs + to the car**
Substitute alternatives for the different parts of speech:
   Here is the **red/blue/little** car.
Expand modifiers into longer phrases:
   The boy/**The tall** boy/**The tall, fat** boy.
Substitute alternative phrase combinations: The dog **that ate
   the cookie**/The dog **that bit the girl** ran home.
Order of difficulty for manipulating terms:
      A.One-two word substitutions
      B.Multi-word substitutions

General Activities: present rhymes, poems and songs;
   begin story book reading.

IV. Themes: Theme Play   14 or over

Read stories and information books to child.
Involve child in conversations and discussions.
Encourage child to tell about experiences and happenings,
   tell stories and say verses.
Encourage socio-dramatic theme play with peers.
Order of difficulty:
      A. From: concrete, immediate and simple events.
      B.To: abstract and general (decontextualized)[b],
         past and future, and complex sequences of events.

[a] Depending on prior experience and development.
[b] Out of context of familiar people, things and situations.

from even limited casual speech, even if it is only to recognize and vocalize a few sounds. In any case, late starting infants are likely to become interested in word labeling play quite readily, and before long will be saying words and forming a few phrases, depending on how well and consistently they are engaged in the language play.

Begin interacting with late starting infants at the *stage* or level of development they have attained, regardless of their actual age — which may be considerably behind the ages shown in Box 4. For example, begin with labeling familiar concrete objects if they know no words or with labeling complex parts of speech (e.g., prepositions and adjectives) if they appear to be more familiar with the easy ones (nouns and simple action verbs) than you had realized. See Chapter 10 for more detailed guidance on how to work with late starting or delayed infants.

Above all, whether starting early or late, don't expect instant progress or consistent gains in language from week to week. It takes time at each stage for noticeable advances in the various skills to develop. Days, sometimes weeks, particularly in the early stages, are often required before the infant grasps a new label; then a whole burst of new terms appears with apparent suddenness. Certain new labels involve totally new concepts. For example, adjectives are a distinct jump ahead of nouns. The infant may have become quite comfortable with learning the names of things (nouns), like blocks, balls, and cars, and be learning new labels quite steadily. But now for the first time perhaps he or she is faced with a label (e.g. adjectives) that represents only selected features of objects, such as round, long, red, and must now learn to separate parts from the whole. Nevertheless, persistent efforts will break through these dry periods of little apparent progress. These are the rewards that make the efforts worthwhile. And actually, the usual course of development is an overall cycle of slow, steady progress alternating with sudden advances.

Baby Explores

Teacher Labels

Figure 4-1 & 4-2. *Taking Turns*

Chapter 4

How to Talk With Infants: Principles of Language Interaction

PRINCIPLES OF LANGUAGE STIMULATION

We have found certain principles in our research to be highly effective in guiding the development of language in infants. These principles are particularly useful to apply in the early stages, before the infant masters language well enough to meet the more complex and open-ended demands of Stage IV. While the thematic activities of Stage IV also make use of these principles, by this time the child's autonomy allows a kind of flexibility that is discussed in detail with the description of the Stage IV activities in Chapter 9. The principles are also particularly useful for working with language delayed children (See Chapter 10), where care and precision in interacting with a child is essential. A skeletal outline of these principles is shown in Box 5.

Interaction

The most important principle is to engage the interest and attention of infants through interacting with them. The process is one of alternately *responding* to their initiatives in exploring and manipulating things and *taking initiative* oneself in an ongoing activity. The idea is to *take turns*, make the activity involving and satisfying for both infant and adult. In this manner, the adult alternately labels the things (i.e., objects, actions, relations, attributes) the child manipulates and the things that the adult brings into the play.

Box 5
Principles of Language Stimulation

Interact with the child.

Be responsive to the child's play initiatives: Label what they use and do as often as you try to label and show them things.

Take turns: Alternate between responding to their initiatives and initiating actions yourself.

Relate personally to the child.

Be warm, friendly, and interested in them and their play.
Praise both effort and achievement: Avoid correcting children's errors (e.g., picking the wrong item); simply demonstrate another time.

Adapt to each child's style (e.g., fast versus slow, playful versus task centered).

Use a meaningful cognitive strategy.

Demonstrate the things, actions and relations you label.

Encourage children to inquire about things in order to engage them actively in learning. Ask them, "Where is the _____?" instead of the more abstract question, "What is this?"

Use several examples for each term to help the child generalize.

Use small objects, with realistic features, which are easier to learn in the early stages.

Pace language stimulation to the child's rate and level of development, and repeat words often enough for them to learn.

Keep the language activities focused.

Use clear speech: Minimize baby talk and use short, complete sentences (more than single words), stressing key words for labeling.

Box 5 (cont.)

Time your actions: Time your labeling to your actions and to the infant's attention.

Use precise labeling: Use concrete, common labels (e.g., carrots in place of vegetable or food) and label things (including different examples) consistently from one occasion to the next.

Engage the child through play.

Encourage children to explore and manipulate toys and other things, labeling and talking about them as they play.

Also involve them in language interaction through social play, manipulating miniature animals, dolls, and other toys as if they were alive.

Play with language for brief 2 to 5 minute sessions as often as possible, and occasionally play for longer periods of 15 minutes or more.

Avoid Over- and Under-directing

A central advantage of teaching through interacting is that it avoids the twin pitfalls of over-direction and under-direction. Over-direction tends to make the infant either resist and lose interest or to passively follow without the active participation and interest necessary to learn. In either case, learning slows, curiosity is stifled and autonomy is discouraged. Under-direction fails to make fully available to the infant the guidance and knowledge of adults that are essential to stimulate language development.

Relating personally to the Infant

Express Warmth and Interest. Close to the notion of interacting, relating personally to the child involves expressing warmth and interest in the infant's comfort, enjoyment, and progress in learning. It is difficult to interact without being sensitive to the child's ongoing needs and interest in the activity and adapting to the infant's styles of activity and learning.

Adapt to the Infant's Style. This means tailoring your style to match the child's way of going about things, whether it be fast or slow, impulsive or reflective, anxious or relaxed, scattered or organized. It also means supporting the infant's efforts just as much or more than their "successes," and praising them by showing interest and enthusiasm in their participation, rather than noting that this or that is "right" or "wrong." It is in fact best to *avoid correcting errors* (e.g., faulting the infant for picking a toy horse when you have asked for a toy cow). They will learn soon enough over the course of successive sessions simply by seeing you label the respective items correctly and repeatedly in the ongoing play.

Be Enthusiastic About Language. Finally, among essential ingredients for interrelating effectively are interest in the subjects being taught, in this case the processes of language and ideas, and enthusiasm for sharing this interest with others. This way you can show that you care that the infant develops and becomes skilled and interested in the mysteries of language and ideas.

Focus on Timing and Precision in Labeling

Time what you say and do to the infant's attention and label each item precisely. Together this focus greatly facilitates the infant's understanding and rate of learning.

Timing: Timing works in two ways. First, it means labeling at the moment the infant is attending to an action, whether it is the infant or the caregiver doing the manipulation; second, it also means timing your initiatives to natural pauses in the infant's ongoing play. The first is key to helping the infant see the connection between language labels and the things they refer to (referents). The second is important for maintaining the child's continuing interest in the play. Poor timing of adult initiatives tends to interrupt the infant's natural cycle of interest in exploring a toy to experiment with the means and ends or social dimensions of what it can do. Such interruptions if too frequent will frustrate infants and make them lose interest in the play.

Precision in labeling: Labeling precision means referring to things accurately and consistently, to avoid confusing the child by using a multitude of different labels for the same item, particularly in the early stages of word learning. Until infants have become fairly accustomed to using a certain name for a given type of thing, (e.g., pig, kiss, red), they cannot easily learn several labels applied to the same type of object, action or attribute. Using shifting labels for the same thing, for example "pig" one time, and "hog" the next, tends to impede the child's understanding of the concept of a word and the functions of labels. It may actually slow the child's rate of learning in the early stages. Even in later stages, when one begins classifying different categories of objects (e.g., fruit, animals, vehicles), a certain consistency is necessary to help the child understand when one is referring to an individual object or to an object as a member of a category.

Using a Meaningful Cognitive Strategy

Because language is not simply a set of specific labels that can be applied literally to a set of specific things, but a complex system of general rules for representing the world in all its complexity, it is important to use a cognitive strategy for helping infants develop language. They must come to understand how language serves as a mental tool for representing and manipulating ideas about the world according to general rules. And they must understand how this works in many different combinations and in any situation.

There are several important ways of advancing these cognitive language skills: one of these is using a *variety of examples* for each word; a second is *adapting your language to the infant's level and rate of understanding*; and the third is *using clear speech*.

Using a Variety of Examples. I have already explained how words stand for things as general types, and not just a single given object. The word for car, for example, stands not just for the family automobile or the child's toy car, but for a type of vehicle having four wheels, seats for passengers, and a motor and other features to make it run. If a caregiver uses the word car to label all cars that the child encounters (different cars on the street and various toy cars) and does the same thing with all other words, it makes it easier for the child to understand that labels are general concepts about types of things rather than just individual names for singular objects.

In the early stages of word learning it is not necessary to draw the infant's attention to the general features that define a car, a sailboat, or a doorknob, and in fact this would require bombarding the child with new

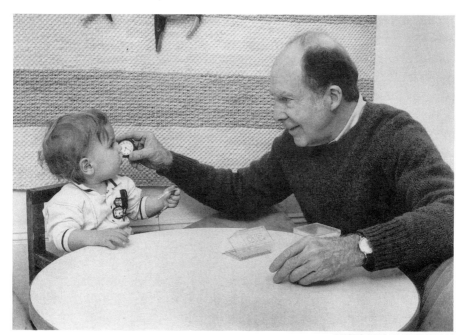

PHOTO BY SARAH PUTNAM

Figure 4-3. *Using Different Examples Helps a Child To Generalize*

words and would confuse the child. Instead, it is more useful to use prototypical examples for each object that reflect the common types of "carness" or "sailboatness" (Rosch, 1973). These general "auras" of the way objects and even simple actions (e.g., kissing, rolling, walking) look, seem to enable infants to grasp the idea of a particular word and begin to apply it to other examples of the same type. It may help at first to minimize the use of bizarre or odd-shaped examples whose features are not readily apparent. Rakish or bulbous modern chairs, racing cars, Irish Wolf Hounds and Chihuahuas, and red bananas may not at first seem to be chairs, cars, dogs, and bananas to the infant. On the other hand, once the infant gets the hang of a word, parents often notice their child overgeneralizing as well as under-generalizing, as when infants call a mail carrier "daddy" or the first horse they see "dog."

Adapting the use of language to the child's understanding. Adapting to the child's understanding is what this carefully graded approach to helping children learn to talk is really all about. Infants who are bombarded with complex conversation from the beginning, without individual attention to sound and word play, are more likely to be delayed in speech development. Begin with simple labels for easily identifiable common objects and actions and introduce only two or three at a time, gradually increasing the number only as the child shows signs of understanding them.

The interactive, play approach (see below) to learning is particularly suited to adapting to each infant's level and pace of progress, as well as to her or his style. The curriculum is determined in a general way by the adult, following the logical order of levels in which language has to be learned, as well as the framework of family interests or the day care program. But many of the particulars of what is learned at the successive levels—choice of sounds, specific words and other parts of speech, and later of sentences and theme content—are in large part determined by what interests the child in these frameworks. The adult labels what the infant turns his or her attention to; additionally, much of what the adult introduces into the play (when all goes smoothly) is based on selecting what the adult knows the infant is likely to be interested in and ready for.

Clarity of articulation. Clear speech contributes to understanding the sound or physical basis for language. Pronounce words clearly, consistently, and not too rapidly (initially), minimizing the use of baby talk. Language, after all, is constructed of sound patterns following certain rules. Blurred or rapid speech makes it difficult to learn the rules for how sound is patterned to construct words. Using a few diminutives now and then, such as "babykins" or "itsy bitsy" will make little difference in the long run. But frequent baby talk becomes almost a special jargon or dialect that gives the infant a poor basis for understanding the speech of others (or for being understood outside the family) and hence for acquiring language as a general tool for understanding and social communication. In day care of course, given the group framework and the presence of multiple teachers, baby talk is unlikely to become a problem.

Engaging the Infant Through Play

Play is the natural activity of infants and young children for exploring and experimenting with the world. It is the process by which children become familiar with the details of their environment and master for themselves the means and end rules about the world they are first exposed to through observation and instruction. Stimulating children's language in the course of their play is thus working in their natural medium, where they are most

Figure 4-4. Exploratory and Manipulative Play

likely to be interested and able to understand.

There are different ways to use language in play, all of which can be applied both when the child is taking action and when the adult is initiating an action. Among the chief activities are: *exploratory and manipulative play* with objects, *experimenting with the means and end of things*, *socio-dramatic play*, and *construction play*.

Exploration and Manipulation. Labeling things in exploratory and manipulative play is likely to be the most frequent form of language play in the early stages of word learning during the baby's first year of life. The process is simply one of labeling various objects and actions as the infant explores them, as well as labeling items when you yourself manipulate them in simple ways appropriate to the child's level.

Play with Means and Ends. Labeling items in the course of experimenting with the means and ends of things is much the same, only the actions are more complex and are used gradually as the baby develops. It is useful to think about learning a repertoire of different things to do with children's toys and everyday materials, because adults can do many more things than infants can to make the play more interesting for them. Many of the means

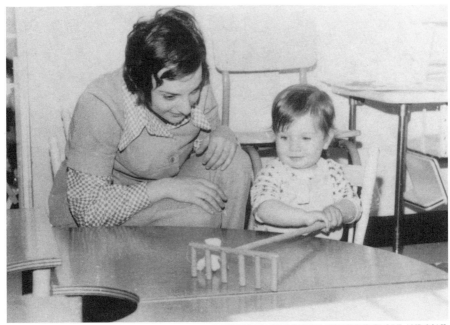

Figure 4-5. *Playing with Means and Ends*

and end actions consist of putting various objects in and out of boxes and containers of all kinds, or simply placing things on, under or behind other objects. Moving things about in all kinds of ways (in rows, lines, sets, piles, etc.), dropping things into containers, and hiding things in and around toys are also activities that readily capture an infant's interest. It is seldom necessary to really hide the objects. Infants' limited understanding of the permanence of objects makes it fun for them to discover objects that are right in front of them, or to find objects only partially hidden.

Socio-dramatic Play. Socio-dramatic play involves pretending the materials one labels are animated and having them perform various human-like actions, such as manipulating a toy kangaroo to ride in a toy car, eat with a spoon, or walk to some different spot. (In the early stages, be sure to use concrete labels like "walk," "run" or 'jump" in place of the vague general term "go.") As in *means and end* play, label relevant items in both the infant's and the adult's dramatizations. Again, the adult will naturally think of many more ways of dramatizing than the infant, but be sure to keep these simple so as to keep the connection between the label and the object or action clear.

PHOTO BY CATHY HOLAHAN

Figure 4-6. Sociodramatic Play

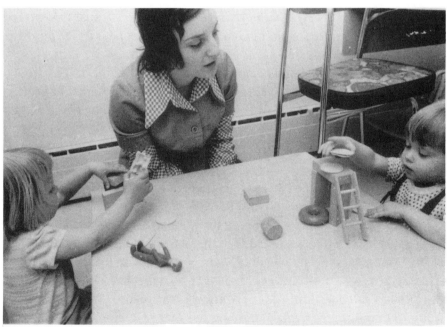

PHOTO BY JACK DOBSON, TORONTO GLOBE AND MAIL

Figure 4-7. Construction Play

Construction Play. Construction play is simply a method of varying the activities to provide more variety and interest to the play. As the infant develops, blocks, boxes and related materials can be piled to make simple "houses," "garages," and other structures. Usually, construction play is combined with socio-dramatic activity, the various toy cars, animals, furniture and other items being labeled in dramatic play along with the construction materials and the buildings constructed. Infants can be easily engaged in manipulating the materials in construction activity, placing a block here and there in imitation of the adult, even before they are capable of piling more than two or three blocks in a tower by themselves.

Figure 5-1.
Table Play in the Home

PHOTO BY CATHY HOLAHAN

Figure 5-2.
Floor Play in Day Care

PHOTO BY RON WOOD

Types of Settings

Where to Talk With Infants: Activities and Settings For Language Interaction Activities

---

Infants can be engaged in playing with words and sentences through almost any type of activity, situation or setting. The more ways used, the more easily and rapidly they will learn to talk. An outline of the chief types of activities and settings is contained in Box 6. They are described in detail below.

Playing with Toys
(Object interaction play)

The Play Setting

Ideally, a well designed and equipped playroom, complete with an infant work table and a variety of toys placed accessibly on shelves, is the preferred environment for engaging infants in any sort of toy play and learning. Day care centers are organized in this way as a matter of course. Even modest or poorly equipped centers will find little difficulty in adapting the guidelines outlined in this chapter. Few families have separate rooms for each child, however, and even when they do, it is important to organize the child's toy environment in some way, keeping many toys in reserve and bringing out selected toys in rotation to keep interest fresh and concentrate focus in play to promote learning. Too many toys within view and reach are distracting. It is also usually more

Box 6
Talking Times and Places —
Types of Activities and Settings for Language Play

Vocalization Play
Interact with infant in imitating and making new sounds for child to imitate in intimate face-to-face contact.

Applies to Stage I. Engage infants during the early months at odd moments throughout the day in any quiet situation in both the home and day care center. Especially adapted to playtimes following meals or during dressing-undressing routines.

Toy play
Label toys and common objects brought into play and otherwise play with language as it develops.

Floor play: In a special corner, or near child's usual play areas.
Table play: At a child-sized table, the child standing or sitting; or in a special seat or high chair placed at an adult table.
High chair: Using chair tray, between meals.

Basic care routines
Label clothes, body parts, implements, and simple actions and otherwise play with language as it develops.

Dressing-undressing: Including diaper changing, preparation and return from outdoors. Also bedtime and getting up routines as feasible.
Washing and bathing: Including hand-and-face washing for meals and complete baths. Use water play toys for toy play.
Eating routines: For both meals and snacks.
Nap and Bedtime: Reading stories and nursery rhymes or singing songs most common. Otherwise engage only in low-keyed labeling activities.

Picture story books and magazines
Label individual objects and actions depicted. Talk about scenes and activities and gradually read and discuss text as language and understanding progress.

Picture story books and magazines can be looked at almost anywhere at anytime, but routine times and quiet corners free from distraction work best. Daily sessions contribute much to cognitive development and interest in learning to read.

Box 6 (cont.)

Social interaction play
Accompany nursery rhymes and other verses and songs with touching, cuddling, surprise games, and physical movements related to the themes of the verses.

Easily fits into many situations at odd moments around the home or during free play routines in day care; most frequently associated with dressing (and sometimes bathing) routines. Useful for all caregivers to cultivate because of its value in developing linguistic competence in sound awareness (which facilitates reading later) and poetry, as well as in fostering intimacy and a sense of fun and drama.

Storytelling and narrating experiences
Telling about things: telling stories, relating personal experiences and recent happenings, and reciting poetry. Begins with descriptions of things present but leads to abstract narration of the past, such as heard and imagined events, conversations and discussions.

Applies to Stage IV: Theme Activities. Telling stories, reciting poetry and conversing are most appropriate for quiet times and quiet corners; they usually grow out of familiar experiences and practices in the home or day care at favorite times and places. Telling about experiences and happenings begins with describing things still seen, or events just observed.

Excursions
Use language to label and learn about things viewed on excursions, according to the child's level of development to extend the child's language and build knowledge about the world. Conversations often develop at mealtimes; discussions may require more planning.

Indoors. "Trips" around all corners of the house/day care center—halls, kitchen, dining room, bathrooms, bedrooms, basement, study, offices, etc.—to draw attention to things the infant does not usually encounter in the usual routines.

Outdoors. Visits to the yard/playground, errands around the neighborhood, routine commuting to and from day care, shopping and trips to the park, whether walking (by stroller or backpack) or by car, and outings to the zoo or on vacations to the country provide further expansions of vocabulary and concepts.

convenient for busy adults and more interesting for dependent infants to play where the adult action is—in the kitchen and other work and activity areas. It matters little which room or area is selected, as long as it is comfortable for both the caregiver and the child and sufficiently free of distraction. Changing the situation or setting for play, moreover, will add variety and zest to the activities.

Toy Storage

On the other hand, whether in the home or day care center, a good selection of toys and learning materials of the type just described needs to be available at the times and places the adult uses for language play. One good solution is to equip a storage cabinet or small set of shelves with a set of language stimulation materials out of the infant's view or in some convenient corner of the children's play areas, or of the adult activity areas (for the home).

An additional solution is to prepare a *portable kit of toys* for current use, easy to take from place to place for play in convenient settings over the course of the day. Suggestions for making up a basic supply and sample portable kit of toys for language play are listed in Box 7.

These toys can be rotated from week to week, drawing on the basic

PHOTO BY CATHY HOLAHAN

Figure 5-3. A Shoebox Makes a Convenient Portable Kit

Box 7
Toy Kits

Basic Supply

Miniature Toy Replicas

Vehicles, boats
Animals and people

Trees, houses and buildings

Lifelike dolls and clothes

Small Common Objects

Tools (hammers, pliers, wrenches)
Food items (staples, vegetables,
     fruits)
Kitchen-dining ware (dishes,
     utensils, pots and pans)
Other household items (scissors,
     clocks, watches, keys, spools,
     thread, string)

Books and Magazines

ABC/picture books (1 or 2
     objects per page)
Pictures of scenes (clear
     illustrations)

Picture books with simple
     texts

Supportive Play Materials

Set of 10 to 15 small cubes and
     blocks (1" to 2" square)
5 to 10 small boxes, round
     containers, paper bags,
     and similar receptacles
A few small balls (1" to 3"
     diameter)
Scraps of colored cloth and paper

Sample Portable Kit

Replicas

Car, truck, bear, pig, cow,
dog, cat, girl and boy

Objects

Apple, carrot, toy spoon, plate

Books

Pictures/photos including
at least some of various
toys and materials

Play Materials

2 boxes, paper bag, small ball,
     piece of cloth

Note: Be sure to include 2 or more examples of each type of replica
and common object in both the Basic Supply and the Portable Kit.
Also include ethnically diverse dolls/miniature replicas of people.

storage supply as needed, substituting new toy replicas (e.g., vehicles, animals) and other common objects to be labeled as the infant progresses and different props (e.g., different boxes, containers, bits of colored cloth and paper) to add interest to the forms of play. A good storage supply and portable kit of language stimulation toys is not so large as to deplete the general supply of toys for children to play with at other times as they wish. But it is enough to ensure that appropriate toys will be available for language play as needed. And because these materials are reserved for times of special caregiver attention, they become particularly inviting and an aid to learning speech. A guide for how to use the basic supply and portable toy kit of language materials is shown in Box 8.

Places to Play

In carrying out toy interaction play for helping children learn to talk, on the floor, in a high chair, or at an infant table work about equally well. The language labeling play activities are essentially the same in all of these situations. It is often largely a matter of preference and convenience.

Floor play. Use an area rug for coziness and to provide an area to focus the activity whether or not the floor is carpeted. A corner of the living room, kitchen, or play room equipped with a small shelf of toys provides additional focus by creating a special spot where language play sessions can be conducted at odd moments throughout the day. For some families and day care centers, regular sessions in the child's room or a special corner of the play room apart from the distraction of other activities may be easier.

In a high chair (or feeding table). Even apart from naming things during mealtimes, a high chair is an excellent spot because the infants are seated in a way that their attention is easily engaged. The table food tray makes a convenient area in which to manipulate a few toys in language interaction play. Infants will often look forward to a few minutes (5 to 10 minutes) of play in the high chair once or twice a day between meals as a matter of routine.

Play at a child's table. Another alternative is playing at an infant table, the infant either sitting in a chair or (when able) standing against the table, while the adult sits on the floor. Special infant seats that hook onto tables of any height can be used with the same purpose, in this case the adult sits in a normal size chair. Again, play on a table surface provides the focus that helps harness the child's attention.

Box 8
How to Use the Portable Toys Kits

General Strategy

Choose two or three replicas and two or three common objects (using 2 or 3 examples of each item) when first starting language play activities.

Use the same items repeatedly in the labeling play until the infant shows signs of understanding by picking up or looking at the items requested.

Introduce additional replicas and common objects (with different examples) one or two at a time, as interest and understanding progress.

Keep the kit at a manageable size by discarding well learned items from time to time, as new ones are added.

The kit is useful for demonstrating language concepts through play in the stages of word labeling, sentence play, and theme activities, changing the materials as the child's skills expand.

Using the Supportive Play Materials

Use the labeling items in manipulative and socio-dramatic play along with a limited selection of supportive play materials (as in the sample kit).

Vary the selection of supportive play materials to add interest to the play.

Label the supportive play items as appropriate.

Using Picture/Photo Books and Magazines

To avoid the distraction of appealing toys, look at picture books and magazines in separate activities, except when comparing pictures of objects with similar actual objects.

Note: Limiting these special kit materials to the daily language play sessions will enhance their appeal and the appeal of the language play.

PHOTO BY CATHY HOLAHAN

Figures 5-4 & 5-5. Gross Motor
Play Provides A Whole New Area
for Enriching Vocabulary

PHOTO BY SARAH PUTNAM

Language Stimulation During Basic Care Routines

When you think about it, much of the infant's day is spent in the necessary routines of child care, drinking and eating, dressing and washing, getting ready for bed, and getting up from naps and a night's sleep. Caregivers who go about these activities as simply a task to get out of the way are overlooking valuable opportunities for love, learning, and personal development. Many others who carry out the routines with gentleness, warmth, and loving care still fail to appreciate how easy and useful it is to engage the infant in cognitive and language learning during these daily rituals.

Practice in language is particularly appropriate because it requires only the human voice, leaving the hands free to perform the needed actions; while the frequent face-to-face contact and physical care involved in these routines combines repeated opportunities to integrate language interaction with intimate expressions of affection. The repetitive character of these routines, moreover, in which much the same set of objects and movements are involved day after day, makes them ideal for learning a basic set of words about clothes, eating, washing materials, and certain body parts and movements. Multiple examples for the same labels are common as well, in the different shirts and pants, portions and forms of food items, bars of soap, towels, etc., and the slightly different ways and circumstances used for carrying out the routines.

Not the least of the benefits from using language extensively in child care routines is advancing children's ability to care for themselves in the personal tasks of everyday living. Talking about the actions and objects while doing them enables caregivers gradually to involve infants in understanding and doing more and more on their own. If busy day care staff and parents can resist pressures to get the task done and involve infants in learning language during the care activities, it will, in the long run, make infants more responsible and personable and create a more pleasant climate of relations as well. Here are some suggestions for using language in the basic routines.

Dressing-undressing and Diaper Changing

The bulk of the task of dressing and diaper changing obviously falls to the caregiver during most of infancy. Labeling the items of clothing and the specific movements of dressing both develop the infant's consciousness about the task of dressing and stimulate language. As understanding develops, infants can routinely be asked to position their bodies, arms, feet, and heads to help with the different tasks. Questions like, "Where is your *arm* (foot, head)?" or instructions like "Put your *arm* in the *sleeve*" and "Let's put the *hat* on your *head*" give daily practice in learning words about the body and clothes. It will take time before the child comes to sort out the different nouns, verbs, prepositions and other parts of speech. But this will come as each type of term is stressed in turn. First comes the simpler labels for clothes and body parts. Closely following are an easy but rich vocabulary of such actions as "put," "zip," "snap," "tie," "button," "lift (your arm, leg),"sit," and "turn (around)." Then come prepositions like "on," "under," and "in" that feature regularly in dressing. Adjectives like "red" hat, "white" socks, and "warm" sweater are also

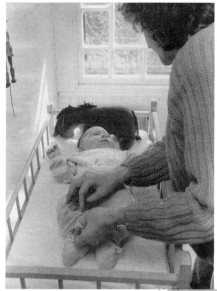

Figure 5-6. *Diaper Changing in the Home*

PHOTO BY SARAH PUTNAM

Figure 5-7. *Changing Diapers in Day Care*

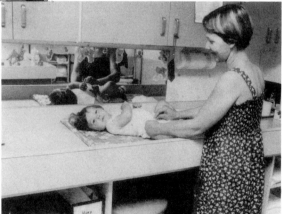

PHOTO BY RON WOOD

PHOTO BY RON WOOD

Figure 5-8. *Getting Dressed in Day Care*

Diaper Changing and Dressing Routines Furnish Daily Opportunities for Labeling the Same Things Over and Over Again

frequently used. When speed becomes important, we may stress an adverb, saying for example "Lets get dressed *fast* today so we can read a story (go to the park, etc.)."

Washing and Bathing Routines.

The daily activities of washing furnish similar opportunities for labeling and development of the infant's language skill and consciousness for self care. Body parts, especially those of the face, hands and arms, feet and

---

Bathroom routines also provide opportunities to use language in ways that promote learning and make daily rituals more interesting

Figure 5-9. *Washing hands in the home*

PHOTO BY SARAH PUTNAM

Figure 5-10.
Washing hands in day care

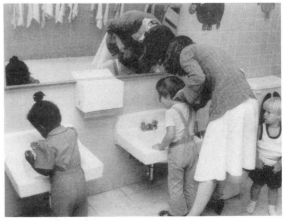

PHOTO BY RON WOOD

Box 9
Talking to Infants During Basic Care Routines

Enhances Caregiver Interest and Motivation by:

Building constructive emotional relations with infants through enlisting their cooperation rationally in accomplishing care tasks.

Engaging caregivers in interesting modes of communication.

Adding the interesting goal of advancing the infant's language skills to the often repetitive tasks of child care.

Making infants easier to manage in the long run.

Makes Infants Easier to Manage and Get the Task Done by:

Engaging infants' attention in learning about language in place of simply running through the necessary rituals of personal care tasks.

Helping them understand and cooperate rationally in accomplishing the care tasks.

Fosters the Development of Coping and Cognitive Skills by:

Establishing the basis for strong relationships with adults.

Increasing the amount of time and attention to learning in activities that may otherwise become boring rituals.

Advancing language skills in activities that promote infants' ability to learn to care for themselves.

Teaching infants to understand and follow instructions in essential social tasks and thus meet social demands rationally.

Teaching them to use language to make their desires known, enlist the aid of others, and initiate activities and thus advance their own cognitive and personal development.

legs, and the different washing tools—soap, washcloths, towels, and water, together with such common actions as wet, clean, wash, scrub, wipe, and dry are among the most common terms readily learned. Color terms, size differences in pieces of soap, towels, etc., and terms like deep, shallow, cold, hot, and warm (water) also come into play, as do prepositions like in, out, on, and under. The common label "dirt," however, may in fact be a bit elusive to the child because it appears in such widely varying and often poorly visible forms. As in dressing, invite infant participation from the early months, gradually asking them, for example, to *rub* their *hands* or *wash* their *face* with a *washrag*, and then *dry* their *hands* and *face* with a *towel*.

As infants learn to sit solidly and safely, opportunities open up for language interaction play in the bathtub (usually more appropriate for the home than the day care setting). A few minutes of play with water toys— floating ducks, fish, blocks of wood, toy boats and the like—furnish occasions for the kind of labeling play used with toys in the regular object interaction sessions on the floor or in a high chair. Prolonged bath routines however, can become a problem. It is helpful to be definite in scheduling the activity, telling the child what to expect in advance, saying for example, "As soon as we have finished washing, we can play with your toys for a few minutes, then we must dry off quickly, to get ready for (lunch, reading a story)."

Eating Routines

Eating activities are much the same except for two things. Labeling is limited while the infant is taking the bottle for formula, milk, or juice and because conflicts sometimes occur in families over food choices and concerns over uncertain appetites, it is important not to let language play overshadow the process of eating.

Such conflicts are less common in day care because of the greater regularization of professionally run routines, coupled with the example that other children provide. The small group context of several infants sitting at a table also makes meals and snacks in day care valuable for involving several infants simultaneously in each labeling activity.

On the other hand, if parents can establish mealtime activities as smooth routines in the home, they certainly furnish a rich setting for language learning. There are plenty of food items (milk, juice, meat, potato, carrots, broccoli, apple and apple sauce, cereal, desert, cookie, etc.), tools (spoon, fork, cup, bottle, plate, dish, high chair, tray), actions (drink, eat, bite, taste, chew, swallow), modifiers (different colors of

Figure 5-11. The home: Language activity in a high chair

PHOTO BY RON WOOD

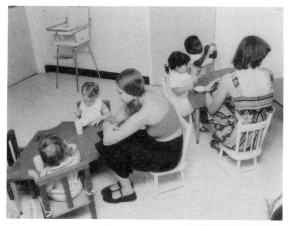

Figure 5-12. Day care: Languge activity with pairs of infants at little tables

PHOTO BY RON WOOD

Mealtimes Furnish Special Opportunites for Enriching Health, Vocabulary and Social Devlopment

---

items, sizes of portions or tools), and relations (in, on) to label and talk about.

Language can be a feature during times with the bottle, but in quite a different way. Nestled in a caregiver's arms, infants enjoy nursery rhymes and other little poems, as well as soothing lullabies and gentle songs that use language in a quieting way. Because the same poems and songs are usually used over and over again, infants become familiar with the words, sound patterns, rhythms, and melodies, all of which heighten their skill and aesthetic appreciation of language.

Nap and Bedtime Routines

Going to bed and getting up each present quite different conditions for using language, whether for naps or for nighttime sleeping—the latter is of course applicable only to the home. Preparation for sleep is a time for low-keyed activity in which engaging the child in the excitement of language play may prolong wakefulness and disrupt readiness for needed rest. On the other hand, many infants are groggy with sleep and sometimes cranky on first awakening, making extended attention to language and learning also inadvisable. Thus, the discussion on stimulation during dressing routines applies more to diaper changes, bathing routines, and dressing for going outdoors and returning home than to those surrounding sleep routines.

Obviously, families and day care staff will want to do what fits each child best, yet a certain amount of verbal communication related to the processes of getting ready for or getting up from sleep, if not too intense or prolonged, is generally helpful. As with other routines, it furthers speech and understanding, and develops both skill and a sense of responsibility that will reap important benefits in the long run. And bedtime stories are time-honored rituals, which when not too exciting are important sources of pleasure and learning. Thus all of these activities, in moderation, serve to further the infant's personal and linguistic development, and make everyday activities infinitely more valuable.

Looking at Pictures in Books and Magazines

Until infants' language is well along, their experience with books centers on pointing to and labeling single objects and simple relations in pictures. It is only when they approach the point of understanding and talking in sentences (Stage III, Chapter 8), usually sometime after the first year, that they can begin to follow a text or even just a story line that connects events from one picture to the next.

Infants who have never looked at pictures may at first encounter some difficulty in seeing a picture as something that represents an object. Even photographs or realistic drawings are flat, two-dimensional depictions of our three-dimensional world. They use such things as shading, depth perspective, and highlighting of key features to make them resemble real objects and scenes clearly. Most infants in our picture-filled modern world are exposed to pictures in some form very early in life. Pictures appear on cereal boxes, magazines strewn around the house, and of course television. Still, following certain simple procedures may help even the

---

**Box 10
Looking at Books and Magazines**

What the Infant Has to Learn:

That pictures represent real things.

How line, shape, shading, size, perspective; and other two-dimensional pictorial rules form pictures of things.

How objects are organized into scenes on a series of pages to develop a story line.

How verbal commentary tells about the happenings and story, first orally, and later through listening to the reading of a text.

The social conventions for looking at pictures, turning pages and listening to follow verbal commentary.

Developing an Interest in Looking at and Listening to Books :

Begin as early as you can, during the first few months of infancy.

Begin with books having clear, realistic drawings of no more than one or two objects per page, then gradually expand to books showing scenes in a connected story line.

First, simply label the single objects, then gradually talk about the scenes in detail, and eventually start reading text in bits and pieces, as the infant's interest and understanding progresses.

---

relatively sophisticated infant understand and enjoy picture books more easily when exposed to them for the first few times.

Things to Consider About Books

The first thing to consider is clarity. The first books need to have simple, clear, and realistic photographs or drawings of objects. It is also better to stick to books that show only a single object on each page so that the child is not presented with a confusing display of things to sort out and identify. Only when the infant has become an inveterate looker at picture books, and gives stable signs of recognizing a variety of different objects, is it

---

Box 10 (cont.)

Look at and label only a few pictures the first session, being sure to stop *before* the infant's interest wanes. Don't be disappointed to spend as little as a minute or two the first session with a child who has never looked at books before, whether the child is only 3 months or is 23 months of age.

Go over the same few pictures for several sessions, until the pictures get to seem like old friends, introducing only one or two new ones each time.

It helps to find a few objects that look like the objects pictured in the child's first book(s), or make a *photo book* like the one described in Box 11.

Label and talk about pictures with interest, dramatizing in ways that appeal to the child, but without over-dramatizing.

Involve infants by asking them to help turn the pages and by labeling/talking about the things they look at as well as commenting yourself.

Look at *information books* and *magazine* pictures in much the same way as you would picture story books, that is first labeling single objects then gradually talking about scenes and reading any text, a bit at a time, as the child develops.

---

time to show picture books with scenes of people and things in action or to include more stylized types of drawings.

Home-made Books

Unfortunately, because such books are not always widely available, it helps in the early stages to make up a book or two to get started. Take a few color photographs of a number of small objects which are familiar to the infant and paste them into notebook with blank pages, one picture to a page. Take the photos with the objects placed against some plain, white or light-colored background so the objects will stand out clearly without

Box 11
Home-Made Photo Books

Purpose

To help younger infants learn the rules by which pictures represent objects by comparing pictures of familiar objects directly with the objects themselves.

How to Make a Photo Book

Cut out a dozen pieces of stiff, white cardboard (about 5" x 8") and fasten them together with notebook rings or clips.

Take color photographs of a few of your infant's toys and small familiar objects around the house, such as:

Toys

miniature replicas, (animals, vehicles, furniture), balls, small blocks, rattles, his/her bottle

Small Objects

utensils, clocks, watches, small lamps, boxes, containers, paper bags, potted plants, keys

Show only one or two objects in each photo, and be careful to place each object against a plain, light-colored background (white, light yellow). Minimize shadows by avoiding glare and using lighting from several directions.

Take two or more shots of some of the objects from different angles.

Paste the best of the developed photographs on the pages of the blank pages of the cardboard "book," two pictured objects on each page: two different examples of each type of object (e.g., two balls, two toy cows) on some pages, and two shots of the same object on others.

Make up two or three such books, selecting the pictures according to themes (animals, vehicles, household items), and keep a kit of the pictured objects for each book stored with the book.

Looking at Photo Books

Follow the same general procedures used with ordinary books, that is, familiarizing the infant with the pictures gradually, dramatizing and involving the infant in the activity.

Box 11(cont.)

Place the objects pictured close to the respective pictures as you look at and label each object pictured, one at a time, presenting objects from the right angle as necessary to help the infant see how it is the same object, and how different examples of an object have the same label.

Shift your focus back and forth between the picture and the object itself, saying, for example,

"Look, here's a key!" (an actual key)...(pause)...
and "Here's a key!" (a picture of the same key)

It is unnecessary to say "This is a picture of the key," or "Here is another key" until later on, as the child begins to get the idea of what pictures are, and can assimilate additional terms.

As with any book, expect that understanding and enjoying the process will take a number of sessions, looking at and labeling the same objects and pictures repeatedly in a leisurely fashion.

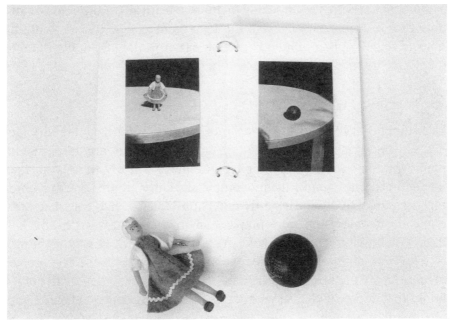

PHOTO BY SARAH PUTNAM

Figure 5-13. Two Examples of Objects Pictured in a Home-made Book

confusing patterns. In taking the photographs, be careful of strong shadows that may distort the pictures. Better still, in place of notebook paper, paste them onto heavy, white cardboard about the size of a book page (e .g., 5" by 8"), then bind about a dozen of these picture cards into a book with looseleaf rings. The result is a sturdy picture book with pages the infant can turn, pull and even mouth with little damage.

Such home-made books not only solve the primary problem of finding clear and realistic pictures of single objects, they are invaluable in carrying out the next step, that is leading the infant to understand that pictures represent real things. On sitting down with a baby for the first look at a book, prepare a kit of objects that resemble the things pictured in the book. When you point to a picture of, say, a toy car on the first page, show the baby an actual toy car, one that looks as much like the one in the picture you can find (which is why the home-made book of photos is so handy). You can repeat the process once or twice, to draw attention to the connection, but don't persist if the baby shows no interest.

Don't expect instant interest the first time you sit a 6-month-old—or even a 16-month-old—on your lap with a book, even a specially designed book. It usually takes a number of sessions, moving slowly a step or two at a time, before babies understand enough to maintain avid interest in looking at a book with someone for even a few minutes. They have to have a number of experiences in seeing pictures to learn all the little rules about how pictures represent objects. Showing pictures side by side with the objects actually photographed makes it easier for them, but it still takes them time to understand what these funny flat things really mean.

Competition with Television

Even looking at TV is not the same thing as looking at still pictures, though TV may be a bridge to understanding pictures. The latter requires mental manipulations to transform things represented statically on a flat surface into action scenes, unlike the movement and story progression dynamics that are perceptually intrinsic to television viewing. It is true that early exposure to television may prepare an infant for understanding and interest in looking at picture books. As is widely known, however, the pull of television animation may become an addiction in itself. The greater mental effort picture books demand makes it sometimes difficult for books to compete with TV, without a good start by dedicated caregivers reading daily to infants, at least as early as TV viewing, and following through until children can read books on their own.

The Value of Early Exposure

If it takes so much time, is it really worthwhile introducing picture books so early, before 18 months or so when they have enough understanding of the world around them to make the leap to understanding pictures easier? It is true that it may take a few more sessions with 3 to 6 month old children than with those 18 to 24 months old, and one may have to proceed a little more carefully and with clearer materials. Yet the advantage of opening up the world of knowledge found in picture books, which in turn is the avenue to the wide world of books, is difficult to underestimate. There are many complicated and exotic things pictured in books—strange and fascinating animals, people and activities, drawings of plumbing and the interior construction of buildings and sewage systems the child can learn about more easily from books than from real life. Exotic people, places, and animals are not easy to visit and interior constructions of buildings and streets are often easier to understand through the simplified schematic drawings in children's books than when observed directly, even when they can be seen at all.

Then there is the endless world of fantasy, story, and information

PHOTO BY CATHY HOLAHAN

Figure 5-14. Getting an Early Start with Books Goes a Long Way to Developing Both Language and an Interest in Reading

available in written material that begins with the picture book experience. The effects are cumulative. Starting earlier establishes a good foundation on which to bring in wider expanses of information, better cognitive skills, and another avenue for expanding the development of language skills.

In many ways it is easier to begin at 3 than at 23 months. Without prior experience with picture books, the older infant may already have developed an active style of physical movement, into everything all the time without the ability to attend quietly and persistently with the continuing concentrated attention looking at books requires. It may be more difficult to reorient the older infant to develop the kind of focused style required for looking at books than to develop such styles in the early phases of development. The problem is one of first learning versus relearning.

As noted earlier, during the first two or three sessions, the infant may not pay attention to more than two or three picture-object pointings, but if you are easy and relaxed about it, over the course of a week or two of daily sessions, most infants will begin to show definite interest. They will want to look at more pictures, will respond when you ask them to point to a duck or a car, will smile and show excitement as you turn the pages, and will want to turn the pages themselves. They begin to feel at home with these little pictures, which become familiar, old friends to be visited and revisited. Many babies develop an interest in a favorite book, as early as the end of the first year, wanting to look at it again and again.

Interact as You Read

The process of looking at pictures in books benefits from using some of the same interaction techniques that labeling real toys and objects in play makes use of. Relate warmly and with interest, involving the infant in the task of turning pages, taking turns in pointing to objects, at first pointing to a cow, then asking the infant to point to it, or "find" it. Above all, show immediate interest and label each picture when the baby points to it first. Timing is again important, though little manipulative play is possible beyond games like hiding (or partially hiding) pictures under one's hand or a piece of colored paper or cloth. Books—even home-made ones—that provide several examples of the same object (e.g., counting books with two pigs, three cows, four hens...) are helpful, not to teach number concepts (at this stage) but simply to indicate the generalizing concept nature of words.

Looking at pictures is thus intrinsically a more abstract type of procedure in which the manipulations are done mentally. It is another important step toward the development of abstract cognitive thinking needed for school learning and modern living. The later phases of this developmental process with books and stories, which depend on children's advancement in absorbing themes in complex scenes and text, will be discussed in Chapter 9 in connection with Stage IV activities.

Social Activity Play with Verse and Song

These are the age old activities parents and nursemaids have played with their babies through the ages. The basic ingredients are physical interaction accompanied by verse or song. Typically, the verse or song text refers to facial features or parts of the body or can be utilized as a basis for finger and hand movements that delight the child. Because they are rooted in sensory motor activity and because they involve repetition of the same sets of words easily linked to body parts and actions over and over again, they are excellent vehicles for both word and sound learning. Face-to-face interaction accompanied by language is a logical extension of vocalization play to more complex levels with words and phrases. Rhyming, when involved, draws attention to the value of individual sounds (vowels, as in the rhyming of "me" with "three") and patterns of sound (vowel-consonant combinations, as in rhyming "sat" with "cat" and "bringing" with "singing"). The added appeal of melody accompanying the verse provides a good beginning basis for musical development.

Among a few of the better known verses are: "Peek A Boo! I see you!" and sometimes, "Do you see me?" as the caregiver alternately covers her/his own and the baby's eyes and face, which when developed into a cycle over many occasions often leads to paroxysms of chortling and laughter:

> This little pig went to market.
> This little pig stayed home.
> This little pig had roast beef.
> This little pig had none.
> This little pig cried, 'Wee, wee, wee all the way home!'

The caregiver accompanies this verse by wiggling each of the baby's toes in turn, starting with the big toe and finishing with the baby toe. Other types of food may be substituted for roast beef.

"This little mouse was looking for a house, and he/she found the house right there!" In this activity, the caregiver walks her/his fingers up the

Box 12
Social Play with Verse and Song

Components

Saying or singing verses to the infant accompanied by physical actions that involve the child, usually with elements of surprise and excitement.

Stimulates socio-emotional, physical, cognitive and language (including sound-poetic/musical) development.

Settings

Often in conjunction with dressing and bath routines, but can be at any leisure moment suitable for intimate play.

Types of Verse Activities

Pointing to and labeling infant's facial features, body parts, and clothes, such as "Where are your eyes (nose). . . ?"

Or demonstrating actions suggested by or described in the verses, usually in ways that involve the infant, such as "This little. . . (wiggling toes in turn) or "Humpty, Dumpty. . . fall (letting the infant drop with your knee)."

Developmental Steps

Start with one-line verses, like "Peek a Boo, I see you!" or simply the first line of "This little pig went to market."

Move to two-line verses, such as the first two lines of "This little pig...," gradually expanding to multi-line nursery rhymes, poems and songs, such as "Jack and Jill. . ."and "There was an old lady. . ."

Repeat the same verses over and over again at each level.

As infants begin to say words and later form phrases, they will begin to repeat, first individual words (e.g. "pig") then phrases ("little pig") soon entire lines ("This little pig went to market") and eventually whole verses of poems or songs, especially if you pause expectantly, ask or otherwise encourage them to repeat the highly familiar verses.

baby's chest or arm, moving slowly, timing the pace to a measured recitation of the words, until the climax is reached with a tickle or a tickling kiss on the neck under the ear. The suspense buildup, over a series of daily sessions, characteristically produces great delight.

Hickory, Dickory Dock,
The mouse ran up the clock.
The clock struck one! And down he/she run!
Hickory, Dickory Dock!

In this case the caregiver runs his/her fingers up the chest to the ear or perhaps to touch the nose, just at the point of saying "struck one," then runs the fingers quickly down again.

Many other traditional nursery rhymes, compiled in many different books and versions, lend themselves to this highly appealing form of social interaction and language play, even though the meaning of them is often obscure to the infant. "Rock a Bye Baby," "Where are your eyes...," Brahms Lullaby, and numerous other little songs are easy to accompany with appropriate movements and indication of body parts to further language and musical development, as well as to soothe, entertain, and develop emotional relations.

Excursions

Trips or expeditions of all kinds are useful for extending the range and frequency of activities involving language. The infant is exposed to language more often and to a greater variety of environments and activities and is made aware of the utility of language in all kinds of situations. At the same time the range of the infant's knowledge about the world and its doings are greatly magnified.

Just what are "language stimulation trips?"

Essentially they are simply taking the infant around the house, day care center or community, labeling the different things and activities seen, both those the infant responds to spontaneously and those the caregiver initiates. The language used should be appropriate to the stage of the child's language development at the time. One might wonder how much benefit infants would derive from activities around the house or day care center beyond their experiences with familiar toys and routines of care, and especially how much they would get out of trips to the outside world.

Like looking at picture books, however, the infant may at first show little interest, but repeated exposure to selected environments over a period of weeks will find the infant showing increasing enthusiasm and responsiveness to more and more details of the different places and activities. These little trips may be divided into two basic types.

At Home: Inside

Excursions around the home are particularly appropriate for the early stages of word learning. There are plenty of different things to point out in the various living areas to enrich the child's vocabulary—bedrooms,

---

Box 13
Excursions

General Strategy

Involve infants in looking at things everywhere they go from the earliest months.

Draw attention and respond to their spontaneous focus on the sights and activities you encounter by labeling and, as they develop, talking about them.

Repeat experiences frequently with the same settings and activities to develop familiarity, language skills, knowledge, and interest.

Avoid carrying children around passively (except when they are sleeping) without thinking about the potentials for them to learn everywhere in the world around them.

Around the Home/Day Care Center

Take them on "little trips" around the house/center and into the yard/ playground (if available) routinely, 2 or 3 times per day.

Label and talk about what you see according to their interests and level, pausing to respond to their explorations and draw attention to the features and functions of furniture, tools and other items you see.

Carry them before they can crawl, then encourage them to crawl and

---

living and dining areas, bathroom, kitchen, halls, closets, and basements inside, and the yard and exterior features of the house outside (depending on the type of domicile). These little trips can easily be started before the infant becomes mobile. The little ones will enjoy being carried in your arms from place to place, as you pause now and then to label what you point to, as well as to what they spontaneously respond to. Once the child begins to crawl and walk, just follow them around on little expeditions. Babies need little encouragement to undertake a journey on their own to the far corners of the house or yard. Just remember to "childproof" all the little nooks and crannies, placing poisons, cutlery, and fragile vases out of reach.

Box 13 (cont.)

walk to new places and rooms once they are mobile, thus combining motor stimulation with language and cognitive stimulation.

Make a game of locating familiar things seen before, asking them to find a "chair," a "big chair," the "sink," a "tap (faucet)," a "screwdriver," the "thing that sucks up dirt [vacuum cleaner]," and other things, according to the language skill level and knowledge they have acquired.

On Errands and Outings in the Community

Involve infants regularly in labeling and talking about the things they see on errands and travel to and from the store, park or day care, whether travel is by car, stroller or carrying the infant.

Make occasional but repeated trips to interesting sites, nearby street construction, house building, the zoo, bus and train stations, and other places.

Read picture books to children telling about things and activities similar to those they are currently visiting, repeating experiences with the books and sites several times.

Don't forget to involve infants in similar ways on vacations and long distance travel.

PHOTO BY CATHY HOLAHAN

Figure 5-15. Excursions Around the Home Offer Many Interesting New Words and Things to Learn

The early indoor excursions are likely to be limited to labeling the different objects (chairs, tables, pictures, clocks, household utensils and tools) and their functions or actions they are used for (sit, eat, see). Later on, once the infant knows a few of the different items, more complex parts of speech can be employed, a step that will no doubt parallel the infant's development in the other types of language stimulation activities of toy play, care routines, and picture books.

As in looking at books, make the first excursions brief and limited to no more than a few items, say, the chairs and lamps in a bedroom. Interest is likely to grow fairly rapidly, however. Infants will enjoy both the extra attention and the new experiences. An additional aid to language learning arises from the fact that many of the objects in these different rooms are simply different examples of already familiar words—new examples of chairs, tables, lamps and other objects. This multiplication of examples broadens the cognitive basis for language development.

At Home: Outside

Visits to the yard (if available), or short visits along the street around the apartment building, are likely to be the infant's first exposure to new and fascinating types of things—the natural world of grass, plants, flowers, trees, insects, stones, sidewalk, and exterior features of the house or apartment building. How new they are will depend on the presence of plants and other natural things in the house or flat and how early the infant has been strolled or driven around the neighborhood. Aquaria and solaria, with their varieties of fish, plant, and other animal life, can provide excellent verbal and cognitive experiences that prepare the child for the wider natural world. In northern climates, the infant's first outdoor experiences may be delayed because of the extreme cold or limited to bleak and snowy winter landscapes. Whatever the case, pointing out and responding to certain features and events in the yard furnishes the same type of pleasure and extension of learning as the excursions indoors, plus the bonus of fresh air, sunshine, and movement in an outdoor setting.

PHOTO BY CATHY HOLAHAN

Figure 5-16. *Snow and Other Seasonal Offerings Extend the Possibilities for Learning about Language and Nature in the Family Yard*

In Day Care

While day care centers may lack the variety of types of rooms and common objects found in many homes, they are likely to offer a greater variety of play spaces, toy replicas, and other toys to learn the names of and learn about. They also offer many more children and adults with names to attach to faces. Also, the better day care centers are sometimes equipped with specially constructed water and earth environments few homes can match. Outdoors, the playground may be specially equipped with a garden containing different natural features to extend language and cognitive learning.

While involving infants in special trips around the center and playground necessarily makes use of the same methods used in the home, infants are likely to learn the names of at least a few things in the course of staff-guided toy play in the different play areas. But not necessarily. Day care centers, like homes, vary widely in the quality of attention devoted to language, as McCartney's studies (1984) on the quality of day care in Bermuda show. Planning little trips around the center and playground, one, two and sometimes even three or four infants on a trip (as they become mobile) can give that needed boost that helps bring language into the daily curriculum.

In the Neighborhood

The first infant excursions are likely to include walks in a stroller, baby carriage or backpack around the block and neighborhood or to the park and playground, often beginning in the early weeks of life. The simple pleasure of movement in a stroller, backpack or carrying sling, the different sights and sounds and the special adult attention will be ample to arouse the child's interest. In addition to the goal of providing fresh air

PHOTO BY RON WOOD

Figure 5-17. Language Play in a Day Care Center Sandbox

and sunshine, adults are often faced with the necessity of taking the child along when they run errands.

Excursions will mean very little to the infant's language development, however, unless they are accompanied by frequent attention to labeling the many things encountered: the sidewalks, cars, trucks, houses, and trees along the way, and the grass, sand, flowers, swings and slides in the park. Many of these things will be added examples of things to extend the child's range of understanding about words already familiar from labeling trips and play about the house and yard. Street, telephone wire, and street light repair, building construction, store windows, the movement of traffic, shopping, and a host of urban or suburban activities will appear here and there to build the child's experiences, depending on circumstances and locale. Repeated walks past street repair sites and visits to the supermarket produce familiarity, depth of understanding and heightened interest. Shopping alone provides endless opportunities to engage the child in increasingly complex labeling and classification of the fruits, vegetables, staples, and other items.

Day care staff sometimes find it difficult to take groups of infants under two on trips around the neighborhood, in part because of liability restrictions by insurance companies. Yet the opportunities for widening the child's understanding are every bit as great for infants who spend their weekdays in day care as they are for children reared entirely at home. Small groups of several infants can easily be accommodated and involved in viewing neighborhood activities, using, for example, double strollers or even wagons holding two infants, with teachers working together in teams. In table play indoors, the advantage of involving 2 or 3 infants together in the labeling and observing process is one of the special advantages of the day care experience.

To the Wider Community

Excursions to the zoo or museums and vacation camping trips to the country are likely to be periodic expeditions, scheduled only occasionally for weekends and holidays. They are also not likely to be high on the family or day care center agenda with children under two, and for this reason will be discussed in greater detail in connection with the theme level of language development for older children (see Chapter 9, Stage IV).

Should young infants of a year or so happen to be taken along, they will nonetheless occasionally respond with delight in certain ways, perhaps calling various strange animals dogs or cats. But taking them often enough to give meaning to the often exotic animals, plants and scientific displays of zoos and museums may be difficult to arrange. Looking at pictures of certain animals a few days before and following a visit will help. Pick out no more than a few distinctive animals to label, such as a giraffe, monkey, snake, and elephant. Go over the pictures several times in a number of sessions and be sure to spend time at the zoo looking at and labeling the same animals labeled in pictures. Depending on infants' readiness, draw attention to the ears, mouth, tail, legs, and other parts to help them see the connection with other familiar animals, as well as to give added experience with familiar terms. The rest of the time on such outings with very little ones is usually best spent simply letting the child look on her or his own, with the adult responding to label what the infant may occasionally find interesting.

In contrast, camping vacations of a week or more may allow enough time for the infant to become acquainted with the local fauna and flora. The place to start is with the trees, stones, insects and similar things the infant is already familiar with from outings in the yard or neighborhood, building on these to extend the child's language and knowledge. Many of the food preparation, eating and dressing activities will also be extensions of daily home routines to new settings and forms. Activities like boating, fishing, water play, walking through fields and woods, and picking berries often relate to prior experiences in the bathtub or looking at picture books, but in any case will widen the infant's repertoire.

Special Excursion Problems: Car Seats, Strollers and Other Infant Carrying Devices

Most trips in modern life are as likely to be car rides as strolls around the neighborhood, with the infant deeply ensconced in a well-buffered car seat. Few people are lucky enough to find a supermarket and other stores close enough for access by foot and stroller, and museums and zoos are rarely close at hand. One of the first things to consider is the advantages and disadvantages of the various carrying apparatuses to both the infant's vantage point for viewing and the ease of face-to-face communication between adult and child. Both baby *carrying slings* and *car seats* are usually woefully deficient on both counts.

In slings the infant is usually carried facing the adult's chest and stomach, blocking both visual and verbal stimulation. Car seats typically isolate infants deep in a well-padded "arm chair," low down in the back seat, limiting their view both forward and to both sides. Verbal and physical interactions with the adult are strained at best. What can one do about these dilemmas? Slings are so convenient during the early months and car seats are not only important safety devices but are widely mandated by law.

While the negative effects of carrying slings may be less important, because they are often limited to the first few months, *there are alternatives.* The infant can be transferred to backpacks once they display strong head and back support and they can be carried in the arms without a sling at least some of the time. Remove infants from the sling from time to time for a few minutes, when on a trip or errand lasting more than a half hour. Interact with them, stopping to look at, point out, and label appropriate things of interest; the plants, flowers, dogs, cats, cars, buses (things on the bus or subway), mail persons, workers digging in the street, etc. Slings can also be re-cut to permit the infant to face outward and to allow the feet and hands to stick out for freedom of movement.

Viewing and communicating from car seats are not insuperable problems either. Some car seats, including the sturdy ones, are designed to provide better viewing perspectives. If they don't, place a small pillow under children to raise them slightly and place the seat near the window or between the gap between the front seats where possible to allow better forward vision.

Car seats for the early months are often designed for the child to ride backward (in which the well-padded seat cushions crash impact better than seat straps). When the infant rides in such a rear-facing seat in the front seat of the car, the infant's eye level is well below the top of the back seat. The advantage this arrangement offers for adult-child verbal interaction and the infant's safety is unfortunately offset by the severe restrictions placed on the child's viewing range in any direction. It is thus best to move to the forward-facing type of car seat as soon as the infant's body is strong enough to handle the impact of seat straps in the event of a crash.

When two persons accompany the child, have one ride in the back seat next to the child at least some of the time to talk and point out things. Or minimize the amount of car travel until the child is old enough to see through the car windows easily and interact verbally from the rear with someone in the front seat.

Backpacks are also far from perfect, but virtually all of them provide an ample vantage point for viewing the passing scenes, at least toward the rear and sides. Some of them position the infant in a way that permits

Box 14
Talking with Infants in Car Seats, Strollers and Other Carrying Devices

Problems with Car Seats

Infants are typically tightly strapped into well-padded seats that narrow their viewing range. (Rear-facing infant seats are even worse.)

Placement of infant seat in rear seat of car restricts easy verbal and visual communication with driver.

Suggestions

Select an infant seat that furnishes an improved viewing range or place a small pillow behind or under infant to widen child's viewing range, and turn your head back slightly toward the child to tell about things.

When possible, have an adult ride in the rear seat beside the infant to talk about the sights along the way in face-to-face contact.

Pad the dashboard to permit placement of the infant seat beside driver.

Problems with Strollers

Height of adult and forward position of stroller restrict face-to-face contact and verbal communication.

Suggestions

Pause from time-to-time and lean over to look at child and talk about the interesting sights.

Stop occasionally at interesting scenes (e.g., street repairs, a garden, a store window), squat down to face child or hold child in your arms and talk about things.

Problems with Backpacks

Rear sitting position restricts infant's direct forward viewing and face-to-face contact.

Box 14 (cont.)

Suggestions

Turn your head now and then to talk about the sights along the way.

Hold the infant in your arms some of the time. It is still the best position for viewing and talking about what you see.

Problems with Carrying Slings

The infant's backward-facing position against your chest severely restricts both his/her viewing range and face-to-face contact.

Suggestions

Carry your infant in your arms at least some of the time so she or he can look around and you can point out things and talk about them.

---

forward viewing. In the better designs the infant is seated high enough to permit the child to lean forward, slightly over the adult's shoulder, to facilitate adult-child communication and furnish a common viewing perspective for the adult to engage in labeling interaction with the child.

Strollers and *carriages* present certain communication problems but not ones that cannot easily be surmounted from time to time. Except when set for a reclining position (for sleeping), they also set the child in an ideal vantage point for viewing just about everything there is to see from all sides. Unlike the car or backpacks, neither the child nor the adult is locked into a position or circumstances that cannot be easily shifted. By leaning over from time to time when something interesting comes along, the adult can easily draw the child's attention to and label a car, big truck, or dog passing by. It is also easy to stop, look and talk about a little bird sitting on a fence or workers digging a hole in the street, for just the amount of time one wants to spend. Moving the infant to one's arms or to the ground for closer viewing takes only a matter of seconds, and is invaluable for easier quality communication.

Figure 6-1. Stage I: Vocalization Play

Chapter 6

Stage I:
Playing with Sounds
(Vocalization Play)

The average infant will begin making various gurgling, crying and other vocal sounds to express satisfaction and discomfort from the earliest hours of life. As development progresses, the variety of ohs, ahs and gahs, buhs, duhs and mms, which are the first approximations of what will later become vowels and consonants, gradually expand. Growth in both the variety and the frequency with which the infant expresses these sounds will depend in part on the infant's general state of well-being, which

---

Box 15
Stage I : Vocalization Play

Learning Activities   **Starting Ages**
Talk with infant in face-to-face contact.   Birth on
Imitate the infant's "speech" sounds.
Make new sounds for infant to imitate.
Interact to get a "dialogue" going.
Order for introducing new sounds:
  A. single vowels and consonants
  B. repetitive syllables (ba-ba, ga-ga)
  C. syllable combinations (ba-da, ka-gi)

Note: Practice with sounds in this manner helps the infant to learn the sound basis for forming words and to establish close emotional ties that foster social and personality development.

means how well his or her needs for food, sleep, comfort, love and sensory pleasure are met. Marked or continued discomfort or deprivation results in dissatisfaction in one way or another, often expressed in excessive crying and various forms of "colicky" distress that narrow down the child's range of responses, including his or her vocalizations.

Establishing a Vocalization Dialogue

But progress in vocalization also depends on the example, encourage-ment, and participation of others. It is here that interactive play with sounds serves its role. The heart of the process is *imitating the vocal sounds infants make*, which they will soon imitate back so that a kind of face-to-face dialogue of continuing imitation between caregiver and baby builds in a spiraling cycle of interaction. The most comfortable positions for engaging in this play is while holding baby in your lap or in a baby seat, your faces about a foot or so apart. If a caregiver engages the baby in this kind of sound play during the baby's waking hours a few times every day, it won't be long before both baby and caregiver have become sophisti-cated players, vocalizing, smiling, and sometimes laughing in an ongoing cycle of pleasure.

Emotional Benefits of Sound Play

Playing with sounds in this way does far more than teach infants about sounds that form the first basis for language development. The close face-to-face interaction involves a satisfying intimacy of relations for both caregiver and child that establishes strong personal bonds and a healthy basis for personality development in the child. And it does so in the medium of verbal communication, ensuring that language will be woven firmly into the fabric of the child's total development.

Adding New Sounds

The next step is to introduce new sounds into the vocalization play, sounds the baby has never or seldom made, or makes only in some vague form. The basis for choosing these "new" sounds is their resemblance to the sounds and syllables of real words. For English-speaking families the new sounds are likely to be certain difficult to form consonants, such as voiced and voiceless fricative (v, z and f, s) and frontal (b, p, m, n) consonants, and short, frontal vowels (those requiring a narrowing of the throat, such as *e* in *get* and *i* in *it*). But because infants vary greatly in the order of

Box 16
Steps to a Vocalization Dialogue

1. Hold the infant in your lap in face-to-face contact.

2. Listen for any sounds the baby makes
                    and
Talk to the child about anything(the routines, how you think he/she feels, etc.) and occasionally make a few single sounds yourself (oo, ah, bu, etc.).

3. Imitate any sounds the infant makes as closely as possible.

4. Repeat the procedures two or three times per day at any convenient time, being sure the baby is comfortable and you talk to him/her a lot.

5. Don't expect the baby to make any sounds during the first few days or to increase the number of different sounds he/she makes in a week or two. It takes time before interaction gets going.

6. *Babies also respond differently*:
   a. Some will smoothly develop a sound dialogue with their caregivers using a variety of sounds in a week or so.

   b. Others will vocalize to themselves when alone, sometimes even by their third month, but be more fascinated with listening to an adult talking and making sounds when with someone.

   c. Still others may not vocalize much at all until they start to put sounds together to try to say words. This is particularly true of babies who are surrounded by a lot of distracting activity or of babies whose caregivers fail to build close and consistent face-to-face relations with them.

7. *But all babies will enjoy this type of communication* during the early months, responding with gestures and excited facial expressions, even if they make few sounds, until learning about words starts to become more interesting to them, usually sometime during their second six months.

sounds they acquire for various reasons, it is best to observe carefully which ones each individual infant is acquiring and introduce new ones accordingly.

As they are learning about sounds, infants begin to understand something about words. As people use words, infants will catch glimpses of the bits and pieces of the meaning and use these understandings to experiment with their first words to draw on the growing repertoire of sounds they can say. In this way the infant's repertoire of sounds is expanded, and equally important, the infant is familiarized in detail with the sound basis for more and more words he or she will soon be faced with learning.

At this stage it isn't necessary to be painfully specific about which new sounds are chosen or how many different new sounds are brought into the vocalization play. At least half of the value of the initial experience is simply getting across the idea that there are a variety of different sounds and that vocalizing sounds is a means of communication. You will find little difficulty in bringing new sounds into the vocalization play, because the baby will gradually attempt to imitate any vocal sound you make, getting the idea that new sounds are to be imitated. As the play goes on from day to day, the infant is likely to imitate more and more sounds and to imitate with increasing accuracy.

Variations: Talking With Infants

Not all vocalization play need be limited to sound play. In the early months, babies frequently vocalize very little and sometimes not at all. Under these circumstances, the caregiver will need to take the initiative and utter a few sounds during the first few sessions to get the baby going. But it can become unrewarding and a bit monotonous to simply make sounds without the baby responding. You may wish to talk to the child about this or that at least some of the time, talking about the routines, about how the baby may feel, or in fact anything at all, as long as you talk gently, naturally, with interest, and not too rapidly. Don't expect the infant to respond during the first session or two. It can take several sessions before an infant really gets involved and vocalizes the first sounds, and even longer before she or he imitates any of your sounds.

Remember, a good dialogue won't develop without establishing an easy and warm relationship between you and the infant. Later, after infants have started to imitate a few sounds, they will enjoy an adult talking to them in words and phrases from time to time, while they continue to "answer" in sound vocalizations. This gives infants the continuing benefit of hearing natural speech in an intimate way and thus more experience in how sounds are patterned into words and phrases. It also helps development of language rhythms and intonations they will make use of in babbling, even before they know any words. But don't neglect the imitative vocalization play. Keep up a regular dialogue of sound play a good bit of the time, along with just talking to the baby at other times. A varying mixture of both will help keep the caregiver and the child actively engaged in the communication process.

You can engage the baby in this kind of vocal play at almost any time of the day, though certain times will work better than others. It is best when you have a few minutes without the pressure of having something else to do and when both you and the baby are relaxed yet relatively alert. Late at night, right after a heavy nap or bed, or just before going to sleep are usually less advisable. Both caregiver and infant may be tired, irritable or less alert, and interactive play may unduly excite both the players, preventing sleep from coming easily.

Figure 7-1. *Stage II: Word Play*

Chapter 7

Stage II: Playing with Words—Labeling Play

As infants become more varied and skilled in the sounds they make, play with sounds and syllable combinations moves easily into labeling the objects and actions of the everyday environment. The words with which we label things are simply *organized patterns* of sounds with the added dimension of *meaning* the child must grasp. There is no need to give up the sound play. The transition from stage to stage should always be gradual. Sound play should continue in the same form for a few weeks, although the activities of labeling are increasingly likely to take up most of the time available for language play. There are other more complex forms of sound play with rhymes and other word variations I shall discuss further on.

Advantages of Labeling Play Over Ordinary Conversation

Labeling play is just what it sounds like, simply naming the common objects and activities infants encounter in their daily experiences. Children can learn to talk simply by hearing people around them engaging in everyday conversation, but the rules for how language works are far easier for infants to learn when their attention is drawn to clear and precise examples that make the individual rules clear to them. Word play is also a form of social and verbal interaction, but the process is more complex than the face-to-face imitative dialogue that develops in vocalization play. Labeling activities can be carried out in many different circumstances and involve more variations in technique than play with sounds does. This ideal is in keeping with the infant's advancing cognitive skills and the wider scope of activities that learning about words entails.

**Box 17
Stage II: Word Labeling Play**

Learning Activities
Starting Ages: 3 months or over[a]

Name things the infant spontaneously looks at and/or touches.
Draw the infant's attention to and name other things.
Order in which to introduce parts of speech:

A. *Simple Parts of Speech:*
    1) small, familiar objects (nouns): hand, cup
    2) concrete actions (verbs): touch, kiss; "up"

B. *Complex Parts of Speech:*
    1) prepositions; in, out, on, off
    2) adjectives: big, little, hot, cold
    3) adverbs: fast, slowly; here, there
    4) conjunctions: and, or, but
    5) articles: a, an; the
    6) pronouns I, you, me, it, we; this, that

General Activities: use greetings, expressions, and simple instructions in ordinary communications; begin picture books.

[a] Depends on readiness

How It Works

The *key to the process* is engaging the infant's attention to an object, action, or event, and labeling it at that moment. In the beginning, it is useful to use single words in isolation, for example, dog or bear when the baby is looking at a toy dog or bear, or bottle at the point of his/her receiving the bottle. However, it is wise and less stilted to use words in short sentences, at least some of the time, saying for example, "Here is your *bottle*" or other label according to the item you are offering. Using sentences becomes increasingly important in familiarizing the infant with the normal, contextual basis of speech as the child advances in learning about words. It helps infants become aware of the complex rules by which words are organized into phrases and sentences (syntax), even before they can understand them. At the same time, it is equally important to *stress the key word* in the sentence for the item being labeled in order to help the infant learn the basic rule that each thing has a specific label (e.g., "Look at the *duck*").

WORDS STAND FOR TYPES OF THINGS, NOT JUST INDIVIDUAL THINGS

Isolating examples that draw the child's attention to rules is one of the principal differences between a productive learning approach and ordi-

---

Box 18
The Advantages of Word Labeling over Ordinary Speech for Helping Infants Learn to Talk

Word Labeling Activity	Ordinary Conversation
Engages infant's attention directly in language and physical activity	Proceeds in the background unrelated to the infant's attention or interest
Is Simple: cuts down the complexity of the language presented to the infant	Is complex: frequently includes words and sentences difficult for the infant to understand
Presented at the infant's level, enabling the child to understand language rules and progress easily	Presented without regard to the infant's level or rate of progress
Is relatively concrete: Relates words directly to the things they apply to	Is relatively abstract: often not clearly related to things talked about
Isolates or stresses key words to make it easy for the infant to understand	Words are embedded in ongoing speech, following the speaker's intentions, without regard to how the infant understands

nary conversation. The latter might be called a "shower bath" approach because it not only fails to isolate and simplify the examples to make it easy for the infant to figure out what the rules are, but also fails to direct language to the child's attention and interests in ways that make it so much easier for infants to learn. Actually, many parents and day care teachers spontaneously do a certain amount of labeling for the infant, but few are sufficiently precise and consistent, and rarely does anyone start early enough.

The importance of using specific labels for specific things has been emphasized in order to make clear how the process of isolating examples helps the infant figure out the rules for what words are and how to use them. But in fact, there is really no such thing as a specific label for each specific thing. Nearly all words are labels for many different examples of some type of thing, such as types of objects (nouns), types of actions (verbs), and types of characteristics of objects (adjectives). For example, the words *chair* and *ball*, and *run* and *touch* stand for all chairs and all balls, and running and touching in all circumstances, regardless of particular features or circumstances. It is for this reason that I have talked about labeling things as a process of furnishing *examples* of things in order to make it easy for the infant to figure out the relevant *rules*. In this case the rule is that each label stands for a variety of individual things that are similar in certain key features (e.g., legs, seat and back for chair), but vary in irrelevant details (e.g., size, color, material they are made of, etc.).

The main exceptions are the names of people (such as Henry or Sheila), including mama and dada, pets (such as Spot or Fido), or other individual things (such as the Eiffel Tower) for which there is only one of a kind. The labeling process is further complicated by the fact that every object is commonly given a number of different labels that are interchangeable according to which category the speaker decides. Thus a dog may be referred to as a dog, an animal, a pet, a cur, or a Collie.

For word play activities, the infant needs a variety of examples for the category of object each label represents in order to understand how words typically work. To further clarify this sometimes difficult point, each word label stands for all things in a category; it is a *general rule* about a type of phenomena, not a label for only one thing learned by rote. The child must grasp the general rule that this word, dog, applies to all things with certain characteristic features (i.e. hairy, four-legged, tail, large jaws), and that every word stands for a different general type or class of objects. Infants must not only label their pet with the word dog, but also their toy dogs, the dogs they see on the street, and the pictures of dogs they see in books. They must encounter numerous examples for all words in order to develop their understanding of what a word is in its most general sense. Understanding that words usually stand for all examples of a type takes time. This is why it usually takes several months after word learning begins before infants can say and use their first real words (see Box 2, Chapter 2. How children learn language rules will be discussed in more detail in Chapter 11).

The Different Parts of Speech Are Labels for Different Things

Objects are not the only "things" that have labels of course. The various actions and processes around us (verbs such as *walk* or *flow*), the attributes of things (adjectives such *red* or *hot*), and different relations between things (prepositions such as *on* or *under*), all have words of different types to label the phenomena. Thus there are many different types of words the infant must learn about, ranging from nouns and verbs to prepositions and adverbs, which are called the different parts of speech. This variation in parts of speech greatly complicates the process of understanding rules about words, because the words for things other than objects are more difficult to interpret and apply correctly.

SIMPLE PARTS OF SPEECH: LABELING OBJECTS AND ACTIONS—NOUNS AND VERBS AGE: 3 MONTHS ON

Because the different parts of speech are not of equal difficulty, as the order in which children generally learn them indicates, it is advisable to start with the simplest parts of speech first (nouns and verbs), and from these categories select the most concrete examples. Start with objects the infant sees every day and has become attached to; research has shown that the first words babies learn tend to be the names of the small things they can readily see and play with (Nelson, 1973).

Nouns

Their own toys, the foods they eat every day, and the familiar small things around the house, such as clocks, books, items of clothing, body parts,

Figure 7-2. Day Care: Even Infants Less Than a Year Old Will Enjoy Language Play in Small Groups

bottles, and the like, are easiest to start with. Things like ceilings and walls are uninteresting objects, too large and vague for the young infant to understand easily and "get a hold of" visually, so they are better learned later on. A list of common things around the home that caregivers in our projects have found useful to begin with is shown in Box 19. This "curriculum" is organized into categories for convenience.

Verbs

Similarly, the simplest and most concrete verbs apply to specific actions the infant can readily see. Since actions disappear once executed, verbs can be elusive; but if simple actions are performed slowly in front of them, infants will learn them almost as easily as the labels for objects. Actions such as *sit*, *walk*, *touch*, *kiss*, *hug*, and *roll* are good ones to start with. A number of useful action terms are included in Box 19.

Action Prepositions and Other Early Forms

A variety of other special action terms (as listed in Box 19) are useful to include in the infant's first labeling experiences. Such prepositions as *up*

Box 19
Suggestions for an Early Word Curriculum

Common Objects (Nouns)			Common Actions (Verbs)[a]		
Care Routines	*Toy Play*	*Excursions*		*Actions*	*Verb-Like Terms*
Eating	Replicas	Home	Community	Specific	Expressions
Drinking	**Animals**	**Indoors**	**General**	**Body**	hi, hello
bottle	dog, cat		sidewalk	sit, stand	goodbye
nipple	cow, pig	furniture	street	lie, crawl	bye-bye
milk, juice	**People**	dishes	house, store	walk, run	thank you
water	mama, daddy	utensils	building	jump, climb	please
Food items	man, woman	(as	sign	**Hand-arm**	all gone
meat, fish	baby, doll	listed	window	touch, pat	**Verb-Like**
vegetables	girl, boy	with	**Vehicles**	push, pull	**Uses of:**
peas, beans	sis, bro	toy	car, bus	hold	*Prepositions*
potatoes	**Vehicles**	replicas)	streetcar	reach	up-down
carrots	car, truck	**Other**	truck, van	pick up	in-out
fruit	bus, boat	**Items:**	**Park**	point	on-off
banana	**Furniture**	various	tree, branch	**Other**	*Adjectives*
pear, peach	table, chair	tools	grass, bush	kiss, hug	hot, cold
apple (sauce)	sofa, rug	key,lock	stone, dirt	eat, bite	big, little
egg, cereal	light, lamp	clock	sand, hole	chew	wet, dry
toast, bread	**Dishes**	watch	flower	drink	*Adverbs*
cookie, cracker	plate, bowl	pen	**Playground**	wash, dry	no, yes
Utensils	cup (mug)	pencil	slide, swing		here, there
spoon,napkin	**Utensils**	letter	see-saw	**General**	
Dishes	pot, pan	stamp	gym	**Purpose**	
bowl, plate	**Clothes**	door(knob)	sand(box)	go, come	
cup (mug)	various	window	**Station**	do, make	
Body parts	**Other Toys**	drawer	(depot)	give, take	
mouth, hand	ball, box	shelf	bus, train	get	
lips, teeth	rattle	floor	track, gate		
finger	block	step,stair	seat, bench		
Furniture	circle	wall	ticket		
high-chair	square	**Yard**	**Airport**		
tray	triangle	grass, dirt	jet, plane		
table	peg, hole	fence, gate	**Zoo**		
bib	ring	stone	various		
	bell, horn	tree, plant	animals		
	crayon	flower			
	paper, book				

CONTINUED ON THE NEXT PAGE

Box 19 (cont.)

Other Care Routines

Dressing   *Washing*

Clothes	**Body Parts**	tub, sink, drain	**Body parts**
diaper (pin)	arm, hand	water, soap	facial features
button, zipper	leg, foot	(bubbles)	head, neck
shirt, pants	head, hair	washrag(cloth)	arm, hand, finger
sleeve, leg	**Objects**	towel	leg, foot, toe
sock, shoe	comb, brush	bath, dirt	genitals and
dress, overalls	scissors		toileting (use
nightie, pajamas			family terms)
coat, hat, mitten			
(family terms)			

(a) What you do in each activity is listed with the "Action Terms" because many verbs are the same for all activities.

and *down*, *in* and *out*, and certain selected adjectives such as *hot* and *cold* are usually easy to comprehend because of their dynamic, highly personalized functional value. In a sense, these first prepositions are really understood as "action terms" by the infant because they represent actions the way verbs do. For example, the infant will want to use *up* and *down* to mean "I want to go up/down" or "pick me up/put me down" and *in* or *out* to tell the caregiver he or she wants to "go indoors" or "go outdoors."

Similarly, the adjectives *hot* and *cold* are likely to be understood first in relation to the respective concrete actions of being heated (burned) by a stove or chilled by an ice cube or a cold wind.

Certain dynamic action terms like *no* (and less often, *yes*), *here*, *there*, *this*, and *what*, along with common social expressions such as *Hi* and *Bye-bye* are listed in Box 19 as well. It is not that these are necessarily recommended words to concentrate on at the beginning stages of word learning. They are in fact somewhat more abstract, but often appear in the infant's early vocabulary because of the frequency with which some families use them and because of their high functional value to the infant.

Special Problems

Baby Talk

Certain forms of baby talk are best avoided as much as possible, while others are almost essential to help the infant master the complex rules of

Figure 7-3. *"That's right! Put the block* in *the can."*

Figure 7-4. *"Now, can you* find *the block?"*

Figure 7-5. *"Can you pull the block* out*?" "Good! You got the block."*

PHOTOS BY SARAH PUTNAM

Preposition: Putting things in and out of containers is an intriguing activity for infants to begin learning prepositions

language easily. The first forms consist of the distorted, cutesy ways of saying things which in the extreme become difficult for anyone outside the family to understand. Fortunately, because day care staff come from different backgrounds and work professionally in group settings, they generally follow more or less common language forms with a minimum of infant-like forms of speech. A few terms of endearment like "babykins" and other diminutives are ways of enhancing intimacy. Using a few alternative labels of this kind will not interfere with language development, but frequent gross distortions of pronunciation can become jargons or dialects that seriously impede the development of articulation skills. When parents also resort to a kind of pigeon syntax, moreover, that is telegraphic forms that omit verb endings, prepositions and articles, for example when a parent says "wan' juice?" "baby wan' go home" or "kitty run sofa" (all pronounced with a slur as well), the infant has very poor models from which to infer what the rules are, particularly if such forms are used repeatedly into the second year. This is not to say that dialects should not be used with infants. They should, if this is intrinsic to the family's culture and form of speech. Dialects are as much a form of language, each with its own complex system of rules, as any so-called standard way of talking.

In contrast, the forms of baby talk many adults intuitively use to simplify and clarify their speech to children in the early years have been widely shown to make it easier for babies to learn to talk (Snow & Ferguson, 1977). These are in fact the methods used in our research, which, when organized systematically, have proved so effective in advancing and deepening infant language development. These consist of introducing the different parts of speech gradually, first using concrete nouns and verbs, and later the more difficult adjectives and other parts of speech. They also include using simple phrases and sentences, pacing the use of variant forms (see below), stressing key terms and relating them directly to the objects and actions they refer to, and employing other simplifying rules that make it easier for infants to learn.

Variant Forms: Noun Plurals; Verb Tenses and Persons; Pronouns

Learning the labels for objects (nouns) and actions (verbs) is not a straightforward matter of using one invariable term for every type of object and action. There are plurals for every noun (except proper nouns) and a range of tenses and persons for every verb; additionally, the verb form must always agree with the particular noun (or pronoun) form used.

Pronouns further complicate understanding because they represent alternative labels for the same examples. They stand in place of nouns. Simplicity and consistency in labeling and syntax will greatly ease the infant's task in learning the first rules about language.

From our research, we have found that the simplest way of handling these potentially confusing shifts in word forms is to initially use singular nouns and the present tense of concrete verbs involving specific actions as much as possible. It is best to minimize the use of pronouns and past, future, and other compound tenses, which are generally too abstract and complex for young infants. Use simple, direct sentences, such as:

You *touch* the bear
I *touch* the bear.

Minimize the use of combinations such as:

He touches the bear
She touched the bear
He will touch the bear
She is touching the bear
She has touched the bear

Learning the different noun and verb forms will come later, through gradually introducing the different forms a step at a time. Initially, also minimize the use of general purpose verbs such as *go*, *do*, and *come*. The actions they label are often less clear and concrete and they typically have confusing irregular verb forms (e.g., *went*, *did*, *came*) that will be easier to grapple with after a few basics are mastered.

Thus, until the infant has learned about 10 words, use labels like the ones below as much as possible (without becoming too stilted):

Use	*In Preference to*	
Singular nouns:	*Plurals:*	*& Pronouns:*
dog, foot	dogs, feet	it, me, he, she, his, her, us, them this, that
Present tenses of verbs:	*Past, Future and Compound tenses:*	
kiss	kissed, will kiss, did kiss, would kiss, is kissing, etc.	
Verbs of specific action:	*General purpose verbs:*	
push, sit, jump	go, come, do	

1st & 2nd person *subject pronouns*	*3rd person* *subject pronouns:*
I/you/we touch	she/he touches (except the plural, "they touch")

You will notice that, in spite of the learning problem that pronouns generally present, first and second person pronouns are among the recommended forms, as in "I/you *touch* the bear." Why not use only nouns as subjects of the sentence? The problem is of course that using nouns means using the third person form of the verb, as for example in the sentences:

The (toy) cow jump*s*,
The ball roll*s*

replace these with the singular form of the verb, as in:

I jump
You roll

Certain variations in the choice of labels and syntactical forms are all but unavoidable from the very beginning. Compromises are necessary. The aim is to introduce the language rules as simply and gradually as necessary, but not at the expense of awkwardness and unnaturalness of expression. Because it is desirable to present verbs first in their simplest form, that is in the first or second person and the present tense (e.g., touch versus touches, touched or touching), it is probably best to accept the complication of the pronouns *I, you* (and possibly *we*) as subjects of the sentence. While they add another label besides their names to designate the caregiver and child, these terms are alternative labels for only two things. The frequency with which they are likely to be used, moreover, makes it easy for the infant to learn the extra labels. Using the "I" and "you" offers a further advantage; they involve the infant and caregiver directly into the play process as actors in the activity. And since the infant's first exposure to "I" and "you" does not demand reciprocity in designating the child and the caregiver, their complexity is minimized. Before the infant can say any phrases, it is always the caregiver applying "I" to her/himself and "you" to the infant.

But it is also desirable to use nouns as subjects of the sentence at least some of the time, in order to provide more opportunities for labeling objects and utilizing them dramatically in play, and thus practicing with the new words in an interesting way to aid learning. This practice can take two forms: (1) Preceding the action verb with an attention directing verb, such as "See the horse *walk*" or "Look at the goat *jump*." Note that the emphasis here is placed on the concrete action verb, indicated by the italics. Because the terms *see* and *look at* will probably be used frequently and be accompanied by interesting actions (or objects) for the infant to view, they are likely to present little difficulty for the infant to understand, even well before coming to use them. (2) Using the third person singular of the verb (e.g, "the doll jumps")in place of the simpler form (using "jump" in some way), which again is a useful compromise.

In the same way, it is also possible to involve the caregiver and infant as actors in the play by referring to them in the third person by their customary names (e.g., *Mama*, *Daddy*, *teacher* and the infant's name), as parents often do. This practice has the advantage of consistency in labeling by using nouns as subjects (instead of pronouns), though it carries with it the complication of using the inflected third person form of the verb (touch**es** versus touch).

Avoid using *me*, *her*, *him*, and *them* (and various possessives such as *his* and *her*) until later, again because of the multiplication of labels and relations. For example, try to say:

You roll the ball to *Mama* (Daddy, Henry, etc.)

instead of:

You roll the ball to *me* (him, her, them)

Above all, be sure to minimize the use of the pronouns, *it*, *this*, and *that* as labels for objects in the beginning phases of word learning. The infant's first task is to learn in some consistent way how to use common labels for things, and these pronouns only appear as additional labels that confuse the child about which name is the appropriate label. Also, their use subtracts from the number of possible exposures to the concrete labels for various things. This prevents the child from practicing the new words. It is particularly confusing when different objects are referred to as *it* (or *this* or *that*) and the infant must keep track of which object is being referred to, while he/she is at the same time trying to comprehend several new word labels.

Finally, remember it is not fatal to use varying labels and complex syntactical forms in the early stages. It merely makes the infant's task of figuring things out more complex.

THE COMPLEX PARTS OF SPEECH: LABELING RELATIONSHIPS— PREPOSITIONS, ADJECTIVES, AND OTHER ASPECTS OF THINGS

AGE: 9 MONTHS OR OVER

Once the baby begins to understand and say a few words, it is time to think about the more complex parts of speech. Often, some of these will have already been used during the first few weeks of the word labeling play, as Box 19 indicates, and one or two of the baby's first words will probably testify. For example, the word *hot* (adjective) sometimes appears early because of the frequent automatic warnings to the crawling infant about a hot stove or radiator. Still, it is easier for the child to grasp the first rules about words if adults stick to the simpler, concrete labels first. This does not mean rigidly adhering to nouns and verbs, but simply concentrating on the easier terms, using relational terms (prepositions) and modifiers (adjectives and adverbs) only when they seem obvious and convenient. The accompanying Box 20 outlines the principal parts of speech and the concepts the child must grasp to use them. The definitions for nouns and verbs are included for completeness.

Move Gradually from the Simple to the Complex Parts of Speech

A short explanation of just how complex terms differ from the simpler nouns and verbs will clarify why it is better to concentrate on the latter before paying much attention to the former. During the first year or so, even well-stimulated infants are heavily absorbed in learning many different concepts about the characteristics and functions of the world around them. If many new functions are introduced in a rapid sequence, they may become discouraged or confused, especially if insufficient time is taken to ensure that they learn each function well before tackling the next one. To learn to use nouns and verbs they must not only grasp the idea that things have a continuing identity and existence (nouns) and that things can move (verbs), but they must also learn to use words to *label* these phenomena, which adds an additional learning task.

　　If we then ask them in the same period to learn to use complex terms like prepositions (in, under, to, from), they must additionally grasp some idea of the positional and directional relations between objects. Yet they are perhaps still consolidating their mastery of the basic notions of object identity and movement. Learning just the basics of spatial relations is a process that stretches over the course of the infant's first 18 months, even for children growing up in richly stimulating environments. Although none of these different functions is terribly difficult, they take time to learn. On the whole, if we let infants become familiar with one or two language concepts at a time in a graduated way, making sure they learn these well before going on to others, the entire process of learning about the world and how to use language to talk about it is likely to progress more smoothly and thoroughly.

Thus, it helps to introduce each new part of speech one or two at a time and avoid labeling more than one or two types in any given activity. Once infants have a few nouns and verbs under their belts, prepositions are a good category to start with. Because they involve relations between things rather than attributes of things as adjectives do, they are sometimes easier to distinguish from the names of the things themselves (nouns). But whether one starts with prepositions or adjectives is relatively unimportant. The difference in difficulty is not great, both are likely to appear among the first words repeated by the child, and it depends in part how carefully and consistently examples are introduced.

As things progress, try not to move beyond prepositions and adjectives for at least the first week or so, or until the infant shows some success in understanding a few of each category, when you can introduce adverbs, conjunctions, and the other complex parts of speech. Even after the child has made progress in a number of different parts of speech, include only a few of any one type or any combination of types during any given language play session. Avoid dousing the child with a long list of unfamiliar terms. You will only confuse or discourage the child.

Special Problems

Pronouns

Learning to use pronouns presents a special problem because of the manner in which they shift their referents (the things they refer to). This is particularly true of personal pronouns, which change according to the roles people play in relation to one another. To realize that *I* is not another fixed name for their mother and other persons who take actions, but that

---

Box 20
The Principal Parts of Speech

Name	What They Name or Describe	Examples
Simple Parts of Speech		
Noun	Concrete objects	cat, ball, pear
	General things	animal, toy, fruit
	Abstract things	love, beauty
Verbs	Actions	walk, kiss, put
	Processes	burn, flow, melt
	Linking verb (copula)	am, is, are, was, were
Complex Parts of Speech		
Prepositions	Positions	up-down, in-out
	Relations between things	beside, behind, near
	Directions of movement	to-from, toward-away
Adjectives	Characteristics of things: (Modify nouns)	big-little, hard-soft
	Comparisons of things	big-bigger-biggest
	Designates which thing(s)	this-that, these-those, what/which/whose (doll/s)

---

they (the infants) too become *I* when they perform an action (and become *you* when referred to by others, and *me* when referring to themselves as the recipients of an action) is a difficult abstraction requiring them to conceptualize different roles (i.e., agents versus objects). For this reason, it is often advisable to leave pronouns aside until later, as they are easier to grasp in manipulating sentences (see Stage III, Chapter 8). Everyday social experience and the limited uses of *I* and *you* in early word play will provide examples that help to plant a few seeds before you attempt to teach them in more extended and precise ways.

It is important to keep in mind that not everything children learn about

---

Box 20 (cont.)

Adverbs	How much (degrees of):	
	Characteristics (adjectives)	too/very (short)
	Actions and Processes	
	(verbs)	(run) slowly/now/there
	How much (adverbs)	very (fast), almost (here)
	Comparisons of how much	more-most, less-least
		soon-sooner-soonest
Conjunctions	Connecting terms, such as for:	
	Adding things	and
	Alternatives	or
	Making exceptions	but, yet, still
	Conditional	because, if, although
	Introducing	
	dependant clauses	that
Articles	Designators of:	
	A specific thing	the
	Any of a number of things	a, an
Pronouns	Word standing for nouns, as:	
	Subjects in a sentence	I, you, he/she, it , we, they
	Objects in a sentence	me, you, him/her, it , us, them
	Possessives	mine, yours, his/hers,
		its, ours, theirs
	Designators	
	(demonstratives)	this-that, these-those
	Interrogatives	what, which, who, whom, whose

---

language (or any other area of knowledge) needs to be taught. This is because once they have gotten a basic idea of some concept, they will go on to learn more examples and sometimes other similar concepts on their own. Thus, after they have gotten the hang of what words are all about, and can say a few words, they will start to pick up more and more words they hear others using in their daily activities. In the same way, when children have learned about nouns and verbs, adjectives will come more easily for them. We call this ability of children to progress on their own *learning to learn*. How well children come to learn new material on their own depends on the quality of the guidance they receive in the early stages, which can give them the mental tools to pick up important things about language on their own.

It is, however, also important to realize that even though early stimulation in language (and other concepts) helps children to learn on their own, continuing guidance is also generally quite beneficial at each new stage of learning. Thus, some of the more complex parts of speech—the intricacies of adverbs and pronouns, for example, and the ins and outs of the advanced stages of sentence construction and theme development (Stages III and IV)—will be more readily mastered through continuing guided language interplay between adult and child.

Pacifiers. Pacifiers, or "soothers" as they are sometimes called, provide comfort to distressed infants and relief to harassed parents. With judicious use they ease the stress of demanding schedules and the inevitable frustrations of both infants and caregivers by providing infants with the sensory pleasure of sucking that serves to relieve tension. They do not accomplish these ends, however, without certain costs, particularly if they are overused. What are these costs and what is judicious use?

Pacifiers substitute immediate sensory pleasure for the experience of effort and the harder demands of reality, and, when used too often, they tend to retard language development. Frustration is the result of interference with the achievement of desired goals. It involves blocked desires for food, rest, tranquility, attention, and active exploration (e.g., touching breakables, climbing), but also involves demands to perform unwanted tasks, such as bathing, napping, or eating disliked foods. Frustration reactions in infants frequently become inflated because of conflicting parental practices (e.g., saying no, then giving the child a cookie a moment later) that lead to intensified demands and tantrums as routine responses. Harassed parents then regularly resort to pacifiers as a panacea to solve all crises and begin to routinely use them to prevent strong emotional reactions or even any expressions of tension at all. Pediatricians may prescribe them the way physicians prescribe tranquilizers, as easy solutions, thus blanketing over problems of child rearing and personal conflicts without devoting the time and effort needed to solve them.

In considering "judicious use," the first thing to understand is that never using a pacifier of any sort will not automatically lead to deep underlying character frustrations on the one hand, or thumb-sucking and buck teeth on the other. Much depends on the smoothness with which schedules and modes of parent-child relations are gradually established in the early months. Even premature babies or infants who start life with

---

Box 21
Pacifiers

Excessive Use of Pacifiers:

- Cuts down time for practicing language skills.
- Shifts the child's interest from vocalizing and talking to sensory pleasure.
- Leads to passive withdrawal in place of active coping.
- Gives only temporary relief to infants and parents from infant frustration and tension without solving underlying problems of child management and development.

When to Use:

- As a temporary tension-reducing device in situations of high infant frustration or fatigue.
- Occasionally, to quiet infants going down to nap or sleep at night.
- During early infancy, the first year or so, depending on the child's development and family problems.

Avoid Using Pacifiers:

- As a routine device for resolving conflicts and relieving tension.
- As a substitute for attention and cuddling care.
- As a substitute for guiding infants' attention toward understanding and active coping with the source of frustration, such as engaging their interest in playing with a toy.
- In proportion as infants develop the mobility, language, and understanding to solve problems and cope directly.

---

difficult births or special physiological difficulties (e.g., incomplete digestive systems contributing to "colic") do not experience chronic frustrations that cannot be handled by means other than pacifiers.

Day Care. It is noteworthy that pacifiers are seldom used extensively in the day care setting even with very young infants, not necessarily as a matter of professional policy. Rather, this is because the general smoothing out and regularization of routines in day care, coupled with the continual availability of interesting self-directed and guided activity, soon cuts down on the frustrations and dependencies that lead to excessive use of pacifiers in the first place.

In the home. In addition to the seldom easy and constant task of trying to provide interesting activities, the secret is balancing adult demands for effort and acceptance of reality by the child with provision for satisfaction of his/her basic needs and personal attention and love. Too much or too little food, quiet, or rest will cause developmental problems (e.g., obesity versus malnutrition, hyperactivity versus passivity). Similarly, attention and love are best for the child when they are directed toward helping infants take responsibility for their own care and learn how to cooperate with others. What they are asked to do should be tailored to their level of development. But development advances best when infants' attention is guided toward the means and ends of learning and the accomplishment of tasks even from the earliest weeks, gradually expanding demands for responsibility and learning as they develop. Pacifiers are thus ineffective child-rearing devices to the extent that they turn infants inward, leading them to rely on passive pleasure and acceptance, instead of learning how to actively cope and solve their problems.

With regard to language development, frequent pacifier use has at least two consequences. It cuts the time available for speech and diminishes the infant's motivation to use speech instead of passive retreat as a coping method. Language is a primary tool for expressing wants and eliciting help from others. Encouraging infants to learn to talk thus advances their skill in active problem solving, leading them to want to seek their goals and make their wants known through speech. Pacifying reduces speech practice time and undermines the goal of learning to talk.

Having said all this it is obvious that effective child rearing is far from easy in an imperfect world with imperfect people, beset by competing demands and crowded schedules, and more often than not living in uprooted communities without the extended family supports and knowledge of child rearing traditionally available to families in the past. Effective child rearing is also necessarily a process that changes gradually but constantly with development: the demands for active coping are not the same for the newborn or the 4-month-old as they are for the 14-month- or the 20-month-old. Pacifiers thus become a needed crutch for parents to cope with lack of time or inability to guide the infant's development as well as they would like. Used at odd moments or at points of specially heightened tension, during unavoidable periods of waiting, or when attempting to quiet keyed up children for sleep, they are useful supplements—as long as they do not substantially replace expressions of tenderness and continuing efforts to engage the infant in active coping and learning to talk, and as long as the infant becomes less and less dependent on them after the first year.

ACTIVITIES FOR STIMULATING FURTHER SOUND DEVELOPMENT: VERSE AND SONG

Once the main focus of stimulation shifts from vocalization play to word labeling activities, stimulating further development of the infants' skills with sounds takes a different form. Vocalization play will have made them familiar with many of the major sound units and syllable combinations of

---

Box 22
What Verse, Song and Social Play with Verse Do for Language Development

Saying Verse and Poems:
- Teaches the sound patterns of language through the appeal of rhyme, beat, and intonation.
- Develops abstract understanding of meaning, metaphor, and imagery.
- Provides the intimacy of face-to-face contact.

Singing Songs and Lullabies:
- Transforms the sounds of language into the sounds of melody and musical patterns and fosters musical appreciation and development.
- Plays down or enhances the development of meaning.
- Provides the intimacy of face-to-face contact.

Using Verse with Social Play:
- Combines the appeal of language rhythms with the intimacy of sensory motor social play.
- Translates meaning into physical movements that enhance understanding.

---

the language. Now their task for sound development is to see how sounds are patterned to form words. They will gain, of course, much of this knowledge from the labeling play simply by being exposed to a variety of words composed of different sound combinations.

Yet there is another separate avenue of language experience that can enhance infants' sound awareness and skills, namely, listening to poetry and nursery rhymes. Special attention to sounds as they appear in words used in verse and song refines skills in understanding and pronouncing words. Children become more sensitive to the subtleties of meaning and sound and improve their aesthetic appreciation of language, perceiving how sound variations in words can influence feelings about ideas. These experiences contribute to their development of phonemic or sound awareness (that is, how words are segmented and composed of component phonemes), which in turn will contribute much to their later success in learning to read. The latter requires knowing how sounds are patterned to form words in order to learn how language is represented (coded) in written form.

At this early phase of language development, before and as infants are saying their first words, simplicity, concreteness, brevity and liveliness are the most important bases for selecting verse and poetry. Three types of activities are useful sources for verse activity during Stage II: traditional short verses used in social play, short nursery rhymes, and lullabies and songs.

Verses presented in social play stimulate awareness of sound patterns in a situation of great personal and physical intimacy, which also aids understanding by the caregiver performing the simple actions of the lines, as in the nursery rhyme, "Ride a cock horse to Banbury Cross..." (where the adult has the infant ride on her/his knee) (See Chapter 5, Where to Talk with Infants).

Many of the short nursery rhymes parents use in social play originate with the Mother Goose and other nursery rhymes handed down through many generations. Simply reading or reciting these and other brief verses in face-to-face contact engages the infant through the sound appeal of words in verse and the social intimacy of the situation, but works on meaning more abstractly since lines are not represented in actions.

Lullabies and other songs render language into the medium of music, adding a special appeal and teaching about sound, meaning, and social intimacy. They will also provide the roots of musical development in an especially compelling manner.

Thus, while these different activities vary in the form of their appeal and the skills they emphasize, they have in common *a focus on the sounds of language* (verbal, musical or both) over meaning and engaging and developing the infant in the process of listening to the sound patterns of language in highly personalized ways. As the infant's linguistic skills advance, meaning will increasingly feature in the process, but will always be integrated into the sound values and rhythmic patterns of language.

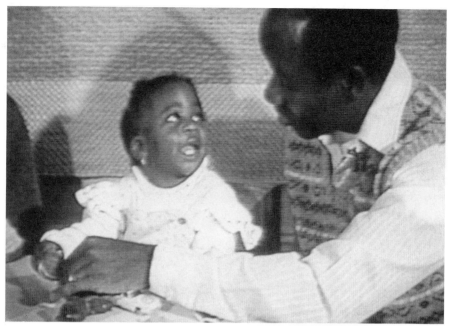

VIDEO PHOTO BY MICHEAL MAJOROS

Figure 8-1. Stage III: Sentence Play

Chapter 8

Stage III: Playing with Phrases and Sentences

Relations Between Word and Sentence Play

Playing with the different parts of speech will lead quite easily into playing with combinations of words in phrases and sentences. In fact, these activities are inevitably closely related, and word play leads almost

---

Box 23
Stage III: Sentence Play

Learning Activities   *Starting Ages*

Combine words into phrases: *daddy + go*   9 months or over [a]
  and phrases into sentences:*Mary runs + to the car*
Substitute alternatives for the different parts of speech:
  Here is the *red/blue/little* car
Expand modifiers into longer phrases:
  The boy/*The tall* boy/*The tall, fat* boy
Substitute alternative phrase combinations:
  The dog *that ate the cookie/*
  The dog *that bit the girl* ran home.
Order of difficulty for manipulating terms:
  A. One-two word substitutions and expansions
  B. Multi-word substitutions and expansions

General Activities: present lots of rhymes, poems and songs; begin books with simple scenes.

[a] Depending on readiness

---

without awareness to sentence play because the full meaning of words is often dependent on the meanings of ideas that can only be expressed in complete sentences. The principles of interaction and the kinds of activities for sentence play are scarcely different than those employed for word play, described in detail in Stage II in the preceding chapter. Illustrating and manipulating larger phrase units still benefit from interacting responsively with the child in play, relating personally, focusing, and presenting the material meaningfully at the child's level of understanding. Nor is there any reason why sentence play should not be equally rewarding in the activities of talking about pictures, responding to the things seen on excursions, carrying out the routines of child care, and interacting with toys in play. No special new materials are needed—using the voice still leaves the hands and body free for the other activities, and as much or as little time can be spent in manipulating a phrase or a series of phrases as is spent in playing with a single word or a string of words.

Thus, in many ways sentence play is merely an extension of word play in more complex forms. I have noted the importance of frequently using words in simple sentences rather than alone in word play, as a means of familiarizing the infant with the way language is actually used in everyday communication, while drawing attention to selected word meanings. The full meaning of a word really only emerges in the description of a process or event of some kind. We do not ordinarily use a word such as *girl* or *cat* without making a functional statement, such as "The girl is running," or "Give the cat some milk." Unless we demonstrate the use of each new word in meaningful statements about actions at least some of the time, infants are likely to learn words in an arbitrary and stilted fashion, and their understanding of the extended meaning that comes out of seeing words used in context will be delayed.

The Role of Sentence Play in Mastering Complex Parts of Speech

This is nearly as true of nouns and verbs as it is of the more complex parts of speech. However, the latter are often more difficult to understand without using them in sentences, because, for example, they apply to relationships (prepositions), attributes (adjectives and adverbs), connectors (conjunctions) and substitute agents and objects of actions (pronouns) that the infant can easily confuse with the label or name of the thing itself. (Nouns also stand for agents and objects of actions in sentences, of course, but they are readily understood as the "name" of an object without having to use them in a sentence.) If, for example, one says *big* or *round* when pointing to a ball, how is the child to know this is not just another name for ball, thus confusing the child as to just what the thing is called? It would seem necessary or at least useful, not only to bring out a big and a small ball to draw attention to "bigness," but also to say something like, "Here's a *big* ball and here's a *small* ball," pointing to each in turn at the moment the key words are stressed. Prepositions (and nouns and verbs) can be confused in the same way. For instance, when putting a toy car into a box, if one simply says *in* during the action without using an explanatory sentence (e.g., "Let's put the car *in* the box"), how can the child know that *in* is not just another name for *car*?

Learning the Roles of Different Parts of Speech

It becomes clear that the new stage of sentence play has actually been going on in some form almost from the beginning. The only change now

Figure 8-2. "The horse is on this box."

Figure 8-3. "The dog is on that box."

PHOTOS BY SARAH PUTNAM

Adjectives and other complex parts of speech are learned more easily in sentences, using good examples

is that the focus shifts to playing with the sentences themselves in ways that involve combining and recombining words in different sentences. The goal is to help the child understand more about the structure of sentences and show how the various parts of speech play *functional roles* in sentences. In teaching about the concept of a word in word play, the focus is on the relationship between the label and the various examples of the item, whether of an object (noun), an action (verb), or of any other part of speech.

In sentence play the central focus shifts to the *roles and relations between words in a sentence*. The child is made aware of how the labels for different objects (nouns), different actions (verbs), and different attributes of objects (adjectives) always have the same roles or types of meaning in a sentence. That is, nouns refer to things that act (subjects) or are acted upon (objects), verbs refer to actions of or upon the various things, and adjectives refer to the characteristics of objects. The child also becomes aware that each of the different types of terms have many possible examples that can actually be substituted for one another—but only within the same category. The play process thus becomes one of running through strings of alternative noun, verb, adjective, pronoun, and other types of labels, substituting the different object, action, attribute, and other labels within the respective types.

Keep the Sentence Play Concrete in the Early Stages

At this stage of language development, it remains highly useful to continue to talk about things in the context of play with various toys and other objects. It is generally too abstract a task for a year-old infant to grapple with examples of how adjectives are used to modify nouns without showing how nouns with these different attributes refer to real things. In the context of manipulating objects in play, it becomes easy for the child to see how an endless string of different adjectives (e.g., red, big, round, etc.) invariably refer to or describe something about (qualify) the things one is talking about (e.g., chair, block, ball) in sentences. Again, the same is true of using prepositions and any other grammatical form.

Needless to say, it is better to start with the simple attributes and relationships the child is likely to be familiar with from daily experience. Adjectives like hot and cold and big and *little*, and prepositions like *in* and *out* and *up* and *down*, as illustrated in Box 19, are likely to have already been used in some way during the child's daily life. Beginning with the

Box 24
Word Substitution Play: How Different Words Can Be Used
for the Same Term In the Different Parts of Speech

Examples of Substitution Strings (to be used with toy animals, dolls
and other objects in dramatic and manipulative play):

Nouns: The baby pats the *dog* (cat, ball, doll).

Verbs: The pig *walks* (runs, sits, jumps, hops).

Prepositions: Can you put the bell *on* (in, under, beside) the box?

Adjectives: The *little* (big, round, square, red) block falls.

                    This (that, these, those) giraffe(s) has (have) spots.
                    This dog is *big* (bigger, the biggest).
                        (Make comparisons with other toy objects)

Adverbs: The cat walks s*lowly* (quickly, softly, gently).
                    Will the cat walk over *here* (there)?
                    The horse can run *slowly* (more slowly, most slowly).
                        (Make comparisons with other toy objects)

Articles: Here is a horse (offering one of several).
                    There is *the* donkey (the only one available).

Conjunctions: Drop the ball *and* (or) the block into the water.
                    Roll your ball *when* (if, after, before) I roll mine.

Pronouns: The cow gives the watch to *you*
                        (me, her, him, them).
                    Put *this* (that, these, those) near the stove.
                    What (who/m) did that cat see?
                    The book is *hers* (his mine, ours, yours, theirs).

more common adjectives and prepositions (and later common examples of the other complex parts of speech) gives the child a good start in learning how they work in sentences. Simple examples of adverbs and other forms of speech are given as well.

Whole Phrase and Clause Manipulation

The manipulation of entire phrases and even clauses as single units represents a large conceptual leap for the child. The infant must now recognize how noun phrases, such as "The big, red ball (rolled down the steep hill)" have the same value in a sentence as the term *ball* alone. In other words, the child needs to become aware of how adjectives, and strings of adjectives, combine with nouns (and articles) to become complete units as the subject (or object) in a sentence. Prepositional phrases, such as "The dog scratched *at the red painted door*" serve the same function as a preposition with a *noun alone* (e.g., *at the door*). Both are objects of the action in a sentence. In the first sentence, *down the steep hill* is similarly a prepositional phrase.

In the same way, the child eventually needs to learn that in a complex sentence, like "The boy who was wearing a red hat ran down the street," the clause *who was wearing a red hat* is nearly a complete sentence that is equivalent to an adjective, such as *big* or *fat*, modifying the noun, *boy*; and it too can be manipulated and substituted as a single unit for other adjectives and noun phrases. Conjunctions, like *and* and *or,* further complicate and expand the combinations and possibilities of phrase and sentence structure, such as *"The toy car and the toy dog* fell into the wastebasket," and *"Either Sue or Mary* can go." In both cases separate noun phrases combine to form expanded yet still single unit noun phrases.

Keep Things Simple and Flexible

Playing with phrases and sentences needs the same flexibility that playing with words does. Keep the examples simple enough for the child to understand, making sure you illustrate what you say with some concrete action as clearly and simply as you can. It may be necessary to say and illustrate an example several times, and in slightly different ways, before introducing another. Avoid introducing too many statements too fast and be sure not to present complex phrases, such as those with two or three modifiers (adjectives or adverbs) and a preposition, before the child shows signs of understanding the simpler ones, such as ones with only one adjective and a preposition.

PHOTO BY RON WOOD

Figure 8-4. *Playing With Words and Sentences Informally in Small Groups Is Likely to Be Common in a Day Care Setting*

Thus, be sure the child has a good idea about expressions like:

The sheep *runs* into the big basket.

before using complex statements like:

The white sheep *runs* slowly into the wicker basket that is under the table in the corner.

Testing Comprehension

In Stage III, you can tell how well children understand your sentences when (1) they begin to imitate reasonably well what you say or do, or (2) when they say or do similar things. More ways of keeping track of children's language development will be presented later on (see Chapter 11, Following the Infant's Progress). Additional illustrations of phrase and clause manipulations, which can be used in play with toy animals and other objects, are contained in Box 25.

The many variations in complex parts of speech (see Chapter 7, Stage II, word play activities) provide endless manipulations with which to

Box 25
Phrase Expansion and Substitution Play

Illustrations of Expansions and Substitutions of Phrases and
Clauses: To Be Used in Sentence Play with Miniature Replicas
of Toy Animals and Other Small Toys

Subject Phrase-Clause Substitutions:

The cow (jumps) =   The black cow (jumps).
                            The little black cow (jumps).
                            The little black cow with the
                               big horns (jumps).
                            The cow and the tiger (jump).
                            The black cow and the yellow tiger
                               with many black stripes (jump).
                            The cow which gives milk (jumps).
                            The tiger with the black stripes on
                               its back (jumps).
                            The cow with the big horns that
                               stick into things (jumps).

Object Phrase-Clause Substitutions:

(The little hen pecks)
on the floor =   in the box.
                            beside the big box near the table.
                            in front of the rubber ball.
                            frequently at the red spot.
                            on the other side of the long box
                               with the holes in it.
                            in the same hole that it pecked
                               in before.

Tenses, Auxiliaries and Other Verb Manipulations
   Present Tense Forms:
      The baby rides = *The baby is riding* (in the stroller).

Box 25 (cont.)

Simple and Past Perfect:
   The baby *has gone* to the park in the stroller.
   The baby *had gone* to the park in the stroller.

Conditional:
   The baby *would go* to the park if the family had a stroller.

Future, Future Perfect, and Conditional Perfect:
   The baby *will go* to the park in the stroller.
   The baby *will have gone* to the park in the stroller.
   The baby *would have gone* to the park in the stroller.

Passive for Active Voice:
   The baby's daddy *took* her to the park in the stroller =
   The baby *was taken* to the park by her daddy.

Further Combinations/Expansions (extended example):
   The last time the baby's mommy brought her to the park,
   which is located on the edge of the city, she was taken out
   of the stroller and put on grass for the first time.

---

engage the child in sentence play in order to further the child's under-standing and fluency.

SPECIAL PROBLEMS AND ACTIVITIES

Activities for Learning Pronouns

Because of the special difficulty pronouns often present for young children, I have downplayed using them during the single word play learning of Stage II. Once the child learns to combine words into phrases and phrases into sentences in various combinations, pronouns become much easier to understand, because it is through sentences that relations between personal pronouns are clearly communicated.

A simple role playing or activity game that helps the child to understand these is for the adult and the child to take turns saying and acting out sentences such as, "I walk to the window" and "You walk to the window" or, "I give the apple to you" and "You give the apple to me." In this way the child is helped to see how the different subject and object pronouns apply to different persons according to the roles they take in a situation. When these singular forms are grasped, role playing games with an adult and two or three children may be useful for learning the *we*, *they*, and *us* forms. Later, possessives (my, mine), demonstratives (this, that) and interrogatives (who, what) can be learned in.similar ways as the examples shown in Box 24 above illustrate.

Care needs to be taken when using pronouns in ordinary speech. It is easy for little learners (and even adults) to become confused over vague antecedents for a string of pronouns in long sentences, such as the following: "She told her to give it to her when she met her."

Advanced Sound Play Activities

Playing with sounds develops a child's ear for language and poetry at any age. The vocalization play of the early months (Stage I) prepares the groundwork for familiarity with the sounds of the native language and how they are patterned to make words. The word-play labeling activities that follow (Stage II) organize the use of sounds into word patterns to which meanings are attached, while playing with sounds continues as a separate activity with the beginnings of verse and song. The phrase and sentence manipulative play that comes next (Stage III) allows experiences with poetry and song to become increasingly sophisticated and complex. As their mastery of sentences improves during the second and third year, infants' earlier dependence on tying what they say to physical action is gradually replaced by the ability to understand and use language in more generalized ways, concentrating on sounds and meaning with less regard for their immediate functional value. They grow to appreciate how sound and meaning are woven into phrasing in broad and complex ways. In the realm of verse this new freedom that develops during the sentence play of Stage III allows them to enjoy playing with the sounds of words in various types of games.

Difficulties in Playing with Meaning

Children also become more and more capable of grasping sentence meaning in longer and more difficult verses and poems. But playing with meaning is a more abstract and subtle process with which more can be done as the child becomes able to tell about a series of connected events in narrative form. Play on word meanings (i.e., puns) are generally too complex for little children. It takes considerable sophistication for them to grasp double meaning variations like *bear* and *bare*, *weight* and *wait*, and block (as a toy) and *block* (as a barrier). They are still too busy working out the boundaries for the meaning of each of the many words they are acquiring to be able to grapple with contradictions between sound and meaning. And obviously having no familiarity with puns based on spelling variations totally escape them. Play with meaning will thus be discussed later with the narrative theme activities of Stage IV.

Expanding Poetry and Song

Stage III is thus very much a period to involve the infant in the varying possibilities of how sounds make words. Playing with sounds at Stage III takes two forms, continuing to hear songs and poetry and nonsense play with words and sounds. There is little to add here to the discussion of Stage II in Chapter 7 about engaging the infant in poetry and song, except to emphasize the importance of reading/reciting poetry and singing (or playing simple records/cassettes *together with the child*) a little bit every day and to bring in longer and more complex pieces only as the child seems to follow them. As always, how well you yourself enjoy the process and are interested in the material will be one of the chief influences on the development of your child's interest and skill. Further details on the development of poetry are presented in discussing Stage IV theme activities (Chapter 9).

Playing with Nonsense Words

Playing with sound patterns by using nonsense words is a particularly useful device for sharpening sound skills. Because they have become familiar with many words and feel increasingly comfortable with handling phrases, deliberately "mis-saying" words is an exciting challenge for infants at this stage. Calling a cat a "scat" or a dog a "nog," a box a "mox" or the child's shirt a "stirt" does not confuse the child. By this time, they know what these common words really are. Infants respond to incongruity and think it funny just the way adults do, provided the alterations are silly, obvious, and based on words they already know thoroughly—and *not* on the play on different real words, that is, puns. The violations of common expectations in harmless ways is the basis for humor at any age. The important thing is not to introduce variations on words the infant does not know or has only just begun to learn. Such mispronunciations will confuse and even dishearten the child's confidence in his or her emerging language competence. Play with well mastered terms strengthens the child's recently established foundation, while play with those only partially learned weakens it.

Nonsense play with word patterns sharpens children's sound discrimination and awareness of the rules for how sounds are organized into words. It thus increases their sense of language control and mastery. It is an excellent basis for developing appreciation of rhyme and verse, and for beginning to establish phonic skills, which is useful for later reading and spelling, despite the irregularities of English spelling.

The game gets increasingly complex as the infant's language progresses. As the child moves into two and three or more syllable words, variations like "nable" for table, "gattle" for rattle, and "spanetti" for spaghetti come into play. A few useful game strategies are shown in Box 26.

What do children do in these games? At first, though they will quickly understand the words to be nonsense variations of real words they know, they are likely to mostly smile and laugh without attempting to contribute original variations of their own. Inventing spelling variations is a complex task for the early stages of language competence, requiring sound and spelling skills that will not develop for some time. Children will need extended experience with games like these before they can begin to create their own nonsense variations. Still, at some point they usually start to invent a few simple variations of their own, such as "gat" for "cat" and "lig" for "big." Even before they reach this point, however, these nonsense games are extremely valuable for increasing sensitivity to sound patterns, which is helpful for later reading, spelling, and poetry appreciation. And soon children will take an active role, vigorously verbalizing disagreement with the adult, saying "No" and before long "No, it's not a mup; It's a cup!" until eventually they are able to present the correct version (e.g., hippopotamus) immediately and repeatedly in the face of an extended series of nonsense mispronunciations (e.g., poppitotamus, tappatopamus, etc.), laughing all the while.

Box 26
Strategies for Nonsense Word Play

1. Multiple variations of a word in a string:
cup = "mup," "bup," "tup," "nup"

When a variation ends up as a real word substitute instead of a nonsense word, as in "mug" for rug, the game spirit need not be lost, as long as the activity is in a context of inventing nonsense words like "nug" and "gug" for rug.

2. Longer and longer misspelled/mispronounced words:

pig = "hig"	mouse = "pouse"
curtain = "purtain"	umbrella = "umprella"
hippopotamus = "nippopotamus"	

The game can get to be lots of fun when the child reaches the point of being able to correct your repeated mispronunciations of a long word, mispronounced rapidly in several different ways like this:

Caregiver:	It's allipator.
Child:	No, it's alligator.
Caregiver:	Is it balligator?
Child:	No! alligator.
Caregiver:	What about alligapor?
Child:	You've still got it wrong! It's alligator!

The child's excitement can build to a high pitch as he or she acquires an increasing sense of word mastery and control in the ability to correct an adult.

3. Several misspelled/mispronounced letters in one word:
hippopotamus = "pipporotamus"

4. Alliterations:
big ball - Tommy table - tiny trains

Concentrate on initial sounds, particularly consonants, building to longer and longer strings, such as:
tall trees—running red rooster—Hal's horse has happy holidays

Important Concerns

Well Stimulated Infants Become Better
Self-Directed Learners Than Less Stimulated Infants

It may be useful to reemphasize that it is not always necessary to set up special activities in order for the child to learn all the rules and intricacies of language—though this does not mean that stimulation from adults is no longer necessary. It simply can take different forms. Once children are well launched in understanding how to use several parts of speech and can combine and substitute phrases in sentences, you will notice that they will use correct terms that they have apparently never been taught. Does this mean that, once well along in making sentences, children can be left to their own devices?

Actually, this "self-taught" advancement that develops gradually in well-stimulated children is only in part a product of the children's own efforts. They are able to make these self-directed efforts in the first place because of special adult guidance. Early enrichment helps them to master better the general *rules* for how language works, which enables them to experiment more on their own. They have acquired a cognitive tool, the ability of *learning to learn* that I have referred to earlier (in the discussion of special problems in learning complex parts of speech at Stage II, Chapter 7). Increasing awareness and skill motivate children to try to figure out additional rules for unfamiliar forms they hear their parents and older children use. They are thus advancing in part from their own experimentation, but also from the stimulation of the language modeling of skilled older speakers—together with whatever continuing special guidance in language and other concepts children continue to receive. The latter will of course generally continue to improve the quality and rate of their development, whether encountered at home or in quality day care and later schooling.

Commonly, even children growing up in less enriched environments eventually are found to start using the plurals of nouns or the past tense of verbs on their own. When they do, from the adult examples they are exposed to, they typically overgeneralize from a regular form. They might simply add an *s* to the singular of *mouse* to make the plural *mouses*, for example, and an *ed* to the verb *go* to make the past tense *goed*. The modeling of background conversation alone has its limitations, however, even at the later stages of early development. Children who have been specially enriched during infancy by attention to learning the rules of language in the ways described here are likely to catch on more easily, cease overgeneralizing sooner (and perhaps avoid the error entirely), and progress further through their own efforts than children whose stimulation has been largely limited to examples of the ordinary adult conversation.

The Social Role Rewards of the Competent Child

But enrichment brings about other advantages as well. Well-stimulated children also continue to progress well because their advancing skills make it easier and more interesting for adults to respond to the children's efforts with continued guidance. Children who succeed are rewarded by more attention in the medium in which they are becoming skilled. Such children assume the social role of "competent child" who becomes a magnet to attract adult attention and praise for his or her successes, thus reinforcing and magnifying them. By the very nature of verbal competencies, moreover, the child is able to engage adults through requests and initiatives in information exchanges and other activities that advance development.

Thus, by simplifying and drawing infants' attention to rules by providing clear examples early in development, infants are given the tools, motivation, and social rewards for understanding language rules and are thereby prompted to experiment more on their own. But, as shown in these examples of incorrectly figured out plurals and past tense, language games that teach the intricacies of language rules can continue to play a role during later development. The special language interaction activities with adults should become more complex, flexible and varied, and adapt to the growing cognitive autonomy and the language stage at which the child is learning, but nevertheless should be continued in some form.

When Enrichment is Discontinued

It is worth mentioning that, should continued guidance be substantially lessened, as occurred to an 18-month-old infant in one of our research projects, the rate of advancement may decline. The mother of this child, upon seeing her boy's high competence in language after he had been in the research project for about 8 months, suddenly decided for some reason that she did not want her boy to become so competent. She wanted what she called "a normal boy." From a baby who at 13 months was rapidly learning new words and even beginning to form phrases, by 18 months both his rate of development and interest in language (and his curiosity and cognitive skills generally) had declined considerably. His ability to construct sentences had hardly advanced beyond his earlier level. Had the mother continued a few months longer, however, the boy would probably have learned enough of the rules to have become more of a self-propelled learner, reaching a level of competence and motivation that would have made it more difficult for the mother and other family members to resist his interest and skilled initiatives in learning.

Fortunately, few families are likely to withdraw attention from their child's language and cognitive development as this mother did, but this example does suggest the value of continuing attention to development. Development is, after all, a cumulative phenomenon. It is the accumulation of many skills acquired through years of stimulation as much as it is the effects of an early start. When better quality language learning occurs throughout development, the child is closer to attaining his or her full potentials of competence.

Figure 9-1. Stage IV: Theme Activity

Chapter 9

Stage IV:
Theme Activities—
Reading and Narrating

Hearing stories and poems read, as well as talking about experiences in simple ways, are part of an infant's life very early in development. The elements of conversing and discussing, too, appear early in simple exchanges during daily routines and various happenings.

Babies introduced to picture books during their first few months in the manner described for language stimulation activities in Chapter 5 will

---

Box 27
Stage IV: Theme Play

Learning Activities	**Starting Ages**
Read stories and information books to child.	
Involve child in conversations and discussions.	14 months or
Encourage infant to tell about experiences	over[a]
and happenings, tell stories and say verses.	
Encourage socio-dramatic theme play with peers.	

Order of difficulty:
  A. From: concrete, immediate, and simple events.
  B. To: abstract and general (decontextualized),
     past and future, and complex sequences of events, outside
     the context of familiar people, things and situations.

[a] Depending on readiness

---

have been exposed to story-like comments about picture scenes and possibly even bits and pieces of story text during their first year. Similarly, infants whose parents have sung songs, read little poems, or engaged them in social play with short nursery rhymes like *Hickory Dickory Dock* will have been exposed to themes in the world of verse, however brief the material.

But theme activities are also rooted in the everyday experience of many infants. Whenever an adult tells an infant about a happening, however briefly, as in the sentence, "Look, Pat (the family dog) is running to the kitchen," the adult is introducing the beginning of a narrative sequence. Because such statements are directly related to common daily events in the family, even the year-old infant can usually follow the story theme as it is expanded to include, "He's going to eat his dinner." And when an infant begins to point to or laugh at Pat slopping his food over the dish, and later say, "Pat 'pill'," he/she has started to converse. All of these diverse activities thus provide infants with their first taste of language developed into narratives of events around particular themes.

Value of Theme Experiences

The importance of developing narrative theme skills lies not only in cultivating the ability to talk to others about everyday personal experiences and immediate events. The value extends to how all of these diverse activities are related to developing abstract thinking skills that are vital for coping with the academic world of school and the complex symbol manipulation of the workplace and other institutions of the contemporary urban community. Children become able to handle language and ideas in a decontextualized way. That is, they can analyze, compare, and organize concepts about completely novel and hypothetical processes and events on the plane of language alone, without regard to their personal experiences. In place of using a small set of familiar expressions and gestures shared by small groups of traditionally bound intimates to express ideas already familiar to all, they are now able to exchange totally unfamiliar ideas in elaborate and endlessly varying verbal forms without relying on gestures at all.

Understandably, mastering such skills contributes much toward the child's readiness for mastering reading, which by nature is built on a code of verbal abstractions. These skills are essential for the child to discuss in the classroom and in strange situations everywhere increasingly unfamiliar ideas more and more unrelated to the child's world of home, neighborhood, and the informal play environment of day care. The later tasks of the adult worlds of work, financial, and community social and political activity are similarly based in large part on these decontextualized verbal skills.

READING TO CHILDREN

Reading Stories

Reading stories to children can become one of the most constant and useful sources of pleasure, especially if this enjoyment is well established during infancy. As a means of stimulating the imagination, giving access to literature and its interpretations of life, providing diversion from life's daily cares, and opening the doors to endless sources of information, the world of books is unparalleled. Books and stories are great multipliers that enrich mastery of language and abstract thinking in many ways. Above all, they develop the ability to follow a maze of events in a logical sequence focused on themes that may be completely out of context of the child's own experience. And of course, reading books to young children is an essential route to reading itself. Many studies have shown a direct relation between the frequency with which young children are read to and their ease and interest in learning to read (Fowler, 1983). An early interest in reading is also important to compete with the animated attractions of television, which often undermine the greater conceptual and imaginative efforts books demand.

The Early Steps

To summarize principles for arousing and maintaining an infant's interest in storybooks (as opposed to simply labeling pictures), start with books illustrated with clear and simple scenes. Talk about them first in limited ways, and bring in the text only gradually, a step or two at a time. Repetition and enjoyment are key. At the beginning, start new books by looking at only a few pictures for no more than a few minutes at a session; then return to the same book many times in increasing depth. Be sure to involve the infants, inviting them to turn pages, point out an action, and as the scenes develop talk about what is happening and what will occur next. In other words, simplification, pacing, and involvement are the centerpieces of the strategy for developing solid interest in and understanding of books.

Getting infants to follow the theme of a story assumes they have already become accustomed to looking at pictures with an adult for the purpose of labeling single objects, as described in the section on word play activities. However, understanding scenes requires the far more complex activity of bringing together a number of objects and creatures (people or animals) in a situation that implies a sequence of events, started in the past and probably continuing into the future. And many times the characters, situations, and activities are only marginally related to the child's experience.

Yet some attention to relations between story characters and events is likely to have occurred with infants who have been already involved in looking at objects in pictures for the purpose of learning words, particularly at the stage of learning the more complex parts of speech. When a picture of a dog running is labeled "Look, see the dog *run*," when two balls are pictured and one is labeled *big* and the other small, or a cat shown lying down is referred to as "lying *on* the chair," we are in fact presenting the elements of simple scenes and stories.

Moving from Objects to Scenes

Advancing from labeling and talking about simple scenes, even unfamiliar ones, is not difficult if taken a step at a time. First introduce books that depict the actions of a single, relatively familiar animal or child over a series of pictures. Each picture should show a character doing a single, familiar action, such as sitting, walking, throwing a ball, eating, washing, and the like. Books of this kind about babies and animals are now plentiful in libraries and bookstores. The infant will progress quite easily from understanding individual scenes to connecting the familiar actions from picture to picture, thus recognizing them as a series of events happening to the same creature. The infant is now able to follow a story line.

Leading the child into more complex, less familiar scenes and activities will also follow, not only easily, but very often with growing interest on the child's part as she or he enters the world of stories. The key as always is not to rush things and to read frequently, preferably more than once a day, but in any case as often as possible. As each new book is introduced, think about its features, particularly what features may demand new challenges to the child's understanding. Do some of the pictures show more than one character in a scene and are they engaged in unfamiliar or complicated activities (e.g., chasing butterflies, driving through a tunnel)? Take time to talk a little about what you think may be unfamiliar territory, and connect it with things he or she already knows. For example, in a story that takes animals into a cave, you might mention

Box 28
Listening to Stories

Steps to Following Story Themes

I. Start with pictures of familiar animals and people in uncomplicated situations. Label and talk about:
- The figures, their features, clothes, tools, and other details in the situation.
- Then their actions, what they seem to be doing.

II. Next find books that depict the same type of animal or human figure in a series of simple situations, some familiar, some less familiar.
- Label and talk about the figure and its features, tools, and apparent actions in the different scenes.
- After a couple of sessions with a book, as you turn to each new scene, begin to talk about and ask the child what comes next and what happened before.

III. By now the child is ready for books with two or more increasingly less familiar characters who interact with one another in a series of gradually less and less familiar events.
- Label and talk about the figures, features, and actions in 2 or 3 sessions before attempting to follow the story line systematically.

IV. Finally, you can begin to pay attention to the text of different stories.
- Start with simple and appealing phrases that point up the actions and events.
- Gradually, bring in more and more of the text, according to its appeal and the child's apparent interest and understanding.

Special Considerations

I. Show the child examples in real life of anything unfamiliar in a story parallel with the story reading activities.

II. Reading stories need not interfere with your continuing to tell stories to pictures if you and the child enjoy it, particularly if you can add imaginative touches of your own.

III. Try to select at least some books that:
- Include children from different cultural and ethnic back grounds.
- Show both girls and boys involved in a variety of domestic, mechanical, adventurous, and occupational activities.

how the child sometimes crawls into his or her cave, the back of a dark closet.

Reading Text

The introduction of text presents a whole new set of demands that the child can master only gradually. Some easy books are accompanied by single words or phrases to describe each scene, perhaps using a verb (e.g., washing, running), but sometimes they use complete sentences (e.g., This is my nose, shirt, etc.). Such descriptions may be difficult to grasp if the conditions described are not readily visible (e.g, It's a warm day, That smells good). One way to help a child to understand obscure points, aside from going over them on repeated occasions, is to demonstrate them. For example, take the child to a very warm room (if the season is wrong for illustrating a warm day); talk about how warm it is and give the child flowers and other fragrances to sample. Real life experiences and understanding stories develop hand in hand, each complementing the other. As children broaden their understanding about real life events, they grasp what is going on in pictures and stories more easily. But as they become sophisticated story listeners, they also find it easier to imagine what unfamiliar experiences are like.

Select Stories with Diverse Gender Roles and Ethnic Groups

Try to look for stories that portray boys doing activities like cooking and taking care of younger children and girls building things and playing active sports. They are not always easy to find in the library or stores even today, but the search is worth the effort. They will widen your child's perspectives about what boys and girls can enjoy and accomplish, whichever gender your child is. Experiences with what are often thought of as the opposite of the traditional responsibilities and activities for each sex help break down the barriers between the sexes by guiding them to share all the things there are to do. Such experiences also encourage children to acquire the skills for activities that interest them and not simply those they are "supposed" to learn because they are boys or girls.

By the same token, it is important to read books to children that include children from a variety of ethnic backgrounds, such as Afro-American, Hispanic, Native American, and Oriental. Surprisingly, considering the years that have elapsed since the Civil Rights movement, there are not as many such books on the market as you might expect. But again they are available and they will do much to help your child understand and empathize with children who "look and act differently" than he or she does. Furnishing positive experiences to your child, at least in the form of stories, will help him or her to appreciate the increasing diversification of cultural groups in American life.

Methods to Arouse Interest

Even books with several lines of text to a page can be enjoyed by infants in the early stages of story reading. The trick is to know the story well enough yourself to talk about the pictures without having to go over the text. As the pictures and story become more familiar to the child over the course of several sessions, the number depending on the complexity of the material, gradually begin to read portions of the text. Start with concrete action statements like "Jerry saw the balloon," ignoring the rest of the text that may describe the scene in more detail. As the child becomes more familiar with the story, add more pieces with each reading, according to the child's level and just how interesting and complex the story is, until you eventually are reading the entire text.

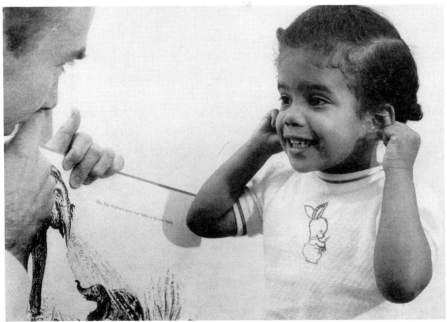

PHOTO BY PHIZ MEZEY

Figure 9-2. *Encouraging Dramatization Is Usually a Sure Method of Involving Children*

While the ultimate test for advancement in the complexity of reading material might ideally be the quality of the child's interest, many other factors often get in the way. Are you sufficiently interested in the story, and do you read with enough clarity and suspense to interest the child? Do you like reading to children? Progress in developing the interests of infants in stories is always a combination of things, including especially the quality of the stories and their presentation. Classics like *Good Night Moon*, *Blueberries for Sal*, and the Beatrix Potter series continue to capture generations of families, both parents and young children alike. When introduced gradually, many of them will capture the interest of infants before they are two.

Many contemporary books for children, on the other hand, including less gender stereotypic ones and those that encompass children from different ethnic backgrounds, can be found with texts at all levels of difficulty. These will help caregivers develop with the child a step at a time. Practice and experimentation by adults will always improve skill, leading to the discovery of appealing elements in even the simplest books, and above all teaching the joys of giving pleasure to children through books.

Reading Poetry

Reading poetry is an important way of deepening children's experience about life, both personally and aesthetically, because poetry combines style and intimacy in very special ways. Further discussion of this topic will be taken up later in this section on theme skills in connection with the discussion on developing narrative skills in children, because poetry lends itself to oral recitation.

Reading Information Books—Science and Nonfiction

Interesting children in reading information books, which pave the way for school learning and the worlds of history and science, is not essentially different from developing their interest in reading storybooks. The primary task in both cases is checking books for the familiarity and complexity of content. The process of gradually introducing more and more complex and less familiar illustrations and portions of the text is also virtually the same. Because there may not be a clear story line to capture the child's interest, however, it becomes more important to ensure that the material is already a little familiar and not too complex. Choose mostly books that seem to cover topics in which the child shows interest.

Figure 9-3. *Pointing to and Talking about the Illustrations Continues to Be an Important Method of Maintaining Interest in the Early Stages of Reading Longer Texts*

Introducing Topics

Animals are usually a safe topic, as they seem to be almost universal in their appeal to children. This is perhaps because animals are usually depicted in children's books in simple activities common to the everyday life of people. But little children also often begin to show interest in various other topics, such as boats, cars, building activities, clothes, dinosaurs or insects, or their interests can usually easily be started. A good way to choose a book about a new topic you'd like to see children get interested in is to first show them something about the topic in real life. Show them a grasshopper jumping, a street being dug up, or a house being built, then select a beginning picture book on the topic. Following through with a series of similar experiences and books to accompany them will deepen the child's interest in the area. Gradualism and follow-through are the keys.

If you follow this course, you'll find you can introduce a wide range of topics, from plumbing and sewing to archeology and plant life, and including those boys and girls don't traditionally become interested in.

Box 29
Working with Information Books

I.   Give plenty of experience with books showing clear and simple pictures of things of all kinds: household items, animals and plants, vehicles, buildings, and tools.

II.   Introduce the child to increasingly complex books and text in the same step-by-step way you use with storybooks.

III.   Find some books that show pictures of things by categories or themes, such as farm animals, desert plants and animals, transportation, and harbor activities.

IV.   Concentrate on a topic area that interests the child or yourself with several books, showing scenes and activities on a particular theme, such as water supplies, distribution and drainage, and household plumbing.

V.   Coordinate book-reading activities over a period of a week or more with real life experiences about the topic, in this case looking at plumbing, hydrants, water mains, and reservoirs.

VI.   Follow through from time to time on selected topics that particularly interest you, developing the theme with a little more depth each time. You are likely to do the best job on the topics you like and know best.

VII.   Try to include a broad range of different topics as well: include themes from different cultures, domestic activities for boys and varied occupational themes for girls, to ensure your child has the opportunity to develop interests in different areas and knowledge of different peoples and ways of life.

That is, by offering girls and boys firsthand experiences in nontraditional boy and girl tasks (boys cleaning house and girls gluing furniture) and activities (boys playing with dolls and girls batting balls), they will look at a new book about girls flying airplanes or boys feeding a baby with

Figure 9-4. *Stimulating Interest in a New Topic: Looking at a Spider in Her Web*

Figure 9-5. *Books with Plenty of Pictures Do Much to Hold Children's Attention to a Wide Range of Topics*

more than passing interest. The same result will occur if you make sure children have a chance to play with children from different ethnic and cultural backgrounds from time to time, encouraging these settings by seeking out play group arrangements in the park or at day care. Reading books depicting "girls doing boys' things" and "boys doing girls' things," and showing children from different cultures, whether in stories or information books, works hand in hand with broadening real life experiences and developing comparative thinking skills. Each complements and reinforces the other to socialize children to experience, understand, and enjoy the world in all its diversity.

Once children reach a certain stage, the process of development takes on a certain momentum of its own, fired by the children's increasing motivation and skill to seek out reading themselves. An interest in books, once deeply aroused, draws children more and more to having them read and soon to efforts in learning to read themselves. Once the "bug" for reading takes hold, children acquire an inner delight and direction and set of verbal and abstract thinking skills that propels them to learn on their own. A rich early start in language, well founded in books, moreover, will do much to minimize the problems of addiction to TV. The guidance process increasingly becomes a matter of background monitoring and serving as a resource agent, steering children in finding gradually more and more complex and vital books. Because the world of topics and the number of books are all but unlimited, while time and energy are forever limited, the value of helping children to plan their time, select books and topics, and engage in discussions about their reading should not be underestimated in furthering children's later development.

NARRATING EXPERIENCES

A number of different oral (verbal) activities, all organizing language around particular themes, come under this heading. One of these is children telling about their recent experiences or a vivid event they have witnessed. A second is participating in conversations and a third is engaging in discussions. Another is role playing activities that depend on language. A fifth is telling stories. A sixth is reciting poetry and a seventh is singing songs. Other variants of these activities will probably come to mind, all of them useful in different ways in helping to form complex, flexible verbal and intellectual abilities in young children.

Telling about Experiences

Telling about things is not necessarily always a formal activity. Children who grow up in highly communicative families that also pay a lot of attention to their children's language development may find it difficult to restrain their child from taking over the language play and telling about everything that happens to them. Given a moderate amount of attention to language, many infants are likely to start telling parents and older siblings about this or that in some detail by the time they are two or two and a half. On the other hand, children in less communicative homes, even if they are stimulated in specific ways from time to time, may come to use language only sparingly, perhaps understanding more than they are willing or able to express comfortably. Children whose families neither talk much nor pay attention to their children's language development, will lag in all forms of language competence. And most children, regardless of their histories, can benefit from a little guidance in organizing and extending their accounts of happenings. How then do we encourage children to narrate freely in some meaningful way without intimidating or discouraging them?

The Early Steps

The obvious place to begin is following some interesting event the child has observed. The time to begin is early in infancy, though narrating becomes increasingly important with development. Experiences important to infants happen to them every day, even before they can say any words at all. Adults talking about their infant's daily happenings both give voice and shape to the child's developing awareness of things and provide models for them to use as their own language develops. Knowing children, being sensitive to their facial expressions in order to read their reactions to events—interest, concern, wonder, or fright—provides clues for what to say to reach their understanding. This helps them voice reactions they are experiencing before they can speak themselves, and will stimulate them to tell about their reactions as their speech develops.

Initially, they will use single words to sum up a situation (holophrases), such as *spill* (for *the soup spilled*), *jump* (for *the dog jumped on the couch*), or *home* (for *mama has come home*). Soon two-word combinations will extend their communications (*soup spill*, *dog jump*, and *mama home* or *mama come*) and then multi-word combinations will follow right along.

Box 30
Telling About Experiences:
Techniques for Developing Narrative Skills

Choose Interesting Places to Visit:

Park	Zoo	Aquarium	Park
Museum	Air Port	Train Station	House Construction
Beach	Factory	Street Repairs	Waterfront-Ships
Lake	Fishing	Pool	Country
Mountains			

Plan Time for Talking about the Visit:

Before the visit — to build anticipation and information.
During the visit — to draw attention to key features and events.
After the visit — to encourage reflection and telling about
    the visit.

**Encourage Talking During and After Errands and
Daily Routines:**

On car and stroller rides to and from errands or day care.
Draw attention to special incidents and activities encountered.

Getting the Narration Going:

Pick a situation free from interruptions.

Ask leading questions along the way, but only as necessary:
    What were the monkeys doing?
    What were the men doing in the street?

Narrow the focus of your questions:
    Ask: What happened to the girl on the long slide?
    Not: What happened in the park?

Avoid interrupting, especially hesitant comments.

Visit with small groups of children occasionally:
    Point your questions toward and respond to the shy
    children often enough to be sure everyone gets equal time.

Scheduling Talking Time

Little by little it becomes possible for the child to engage in connected discourse, to string phrases and crude sentences together, however haltingly, and to tell about something that has occurred. The adult's task is largely one of arranging comfortable circumstances often enough for the child to want to tell about things. This is not always easy in a schedule of busy home agendas and day care programs. It may help to allocate time for reflection and talk following interesting events or personal happenings. Since several usually occur every day, simply pick one or two that come at convenient times and are likely to be interesting to the child.

To some adults, every day may seem too rushed to permit the luxury of "talk time." But daily or periodic trips, to the park, the supermarket, the train station, the airport, the doctor, and even the daily commute to and from the day care center are all events of potential child interest. If there is time for stroller rides or play in the park, plan time (five minutes or so) for talk following the event before beginning the next item on the agenda, even if you need to cut short the outing itself by a few minutes. For parents, arriving home from the day care center may be a hectic time, but car, bus, or stroller rides to and from day care, the park, shopping or errands provide ample scheduled, sometimes otherwise unused, time for encouraging the child to talk about things.

There is also no reason not to talk about the sights and goings-on along the way. By the time children are using sentences fairly freely, their attention span and knowledge are sufficiently developed to go beyond the simple word labeling and brief phrases of the early stages and enjoy the theme activities of Stage IV. They will attend to lengthier comments and explanations about street and telephone line repairs, traffic jams, building construction activities, trees and flowers, running dogs and racing bicyclists. At the same time, remember that the goal is to foster broad narrative and discussion skills in the child, gradually about more and more general topics, not simply to help children say a personal word or two or to teach them about things. Encourage children to talk by responding to their spontaneous questions and comments, even their briefest words and other signs of interest, and by tailoring what you say to what interests them.

Finding Cues
to Arouse Interest

Readiness and receptivity for listening are not always enough to get a child going, particularly when events are embedded in daily routines that seem to arouse little interest to talk about. Think about cues that will trigger interest. Knowing the environment and the child enables one to realize what may be of interest, and to ask leading questions that will arouse new curiosity and talk. The problem centers on identifying what is particularly interesting to children on an excursion (from the home or day care center): a ride in the big swing or down the long slide, the demolition of a building, a huge crowd in a store, a visit to a special variety store, the way the elephant eats or the leopard leaps at the zoo. Periodic visits of parents to the child's day care center to get firsthand images of his or her playmates, their interests, the child's daily routine, and interchanges with a day care teacher at the end of the day can also keep one tuned in to what is going on.

Providing cues works best by *asking pointed rather than open-ended questions*. Asking young children "What happened at day care/home (in the park, store, zoo) today?" places the entire burden on them to recall and organize their thoughts. On the other hand, asking what they did with _____ (name of a frequent playmate) today, what toys they played with, what things they did in the park, what they had for breakfast, or what happened in the meat department, anchors the focus on specifics, reminding them of their little achievements, activities they enjoyed, or things that seemed funny or interesting to them. Narrowing down topics also makes it easier for children to find the right words.

Again, it is important to look for cues for how to respond from children's spontaneous, often half-formed comments about what they themselves observe. Ask questions directly related to what they say, rather than starting off on a new tangent because you think it is more important. Be careful not to interrupt too often by trying to expand what they say, and let them work out their own thoughts.

Working in Small Groups

Children's interest and skill in narrating often develop best in small groups, which are of course easier for day care staff than parents to arrange. Talking about things with other children who share similar skills and interests (their peers) stimulates them to share their ideas and feelings. For this reason, the day care setting is in some ways an ideal environment for fostering narrative and discussion skills. One-to-one relations between adult and child may produce wonders (assuming warmth, flexibility and imagination). But obvious differences in skill, power, and interests may sometimes limit children's efforts, enjoyment, and scope of expression. The greater initiative and skill of one child telling about something inspires the others to make efforts, provided this child is not too aggressive or overpowering in language and cognitive skills relative to the other children. Even then such differences can be mediated by negotiating rules about taking turns and by setting an example of responding with interest to each child's contribution and encouraging his or her development through judicious question asking.

Given regular opportunities during late infancy and the preschool years to tell about happenings in a guided and warm atmosphere, talking about things develops a momentum of its own. Encouragement and practice develop children's narrating skills, making what they say better organized, more selective and dramatic, and more interesting to others. The increased interest of others further stimulates their desire to recount, to become a good storyteller or reporter of events. Like any other skill learned well, performing it becomes a satisfying social role offering the reward of being considered competent by others, and leading one to perform spontaneously and strive for further excellence.

Conversations

Conversing, or "just talking about things," is perhaps the most common way people use language. Although often trivial, the exchange of bits of information to get a task done or the expression of feelings and small talk about daily experiences is a root process for developing narrative skills. At its best, talking informally about various topics sometimes leads to serious discussion about general problems, especially in day care or neighborhood groups among children whose home lives vary considerably. But serious or trivial, conversations frequently furnish opportunities for participants to give accounts about happenings. There is a ready audience prepared to hear some brief storylike report of an experience or event, and sometimes a series of events. In this way conversations provide a good setting for building skills in telling about experiences and telling stories (see below).

Once again, the day care center is an easy social setting for adults to promote conversational skills in children. Teachers have only to be easy in chatting with children, at mealtimes, or during odd moments of their play, preferably with 2 or 3 children in a little corner, away from vigorous activity. Ask a key question from time to time to keep the small talk going and involve the different children. Extended conversations (and discussions) require only a little more time and planning.

With a little thought, planning and attention to arrangements, the

Box 31
Guiding Conversations and Discussions

Conversing   *Discussing*

Arranging a Time and Place

Easiest at sit-down meals: At meals or quiet get-togethers
Plan at least 2 or 3 unhurried   Schedule enough time to explore topic
meals each week, with both
children and adults present

Making Them Work

Set up a relaxed atmosphere: Announce the purpose or topic,
  Expect good conversations only   possibly in advance
  with good food and good moods   Agree to certain rules, such as:
Ensure everyone's participation,   -staying on topic
  including shy and less verbal   -accepting moderator decisions
  younger children   -taking turns: less than 3 min each
Restrain talkative or dominating   -rotating moderators
  individuals   Have participants do a little
Try to encourage topics of   advance preparation, such as:
  -General interest   -a little reading (as appropriate
  -Interest to each person in turn   for the person's skills)
  -High interest—but not highly charged   -asking someone familiar with
                                          a topic
                                          -preparing what they want to say
                                          (about their case/the topic)

How to Mediate

1) Involve quiet/younger less verbal members by:
   a) Asking/introducing questions/topics of personal interest
   b) Suggesting turn taking if needed

2) Discourage talkative/dominating members by:
   a) Shifting conversation to topics of less interest to them
   b) Discussing with them privately how their style discourages the
   quiet/less verbal members

home can be equally effective as a setting for telling about something in
an elaborate organized theme. Remember that people are expected to take
turns and allow other parties to inject a point or mention a related incident

in the course of any telling. Yet conversations also tend to ebb and flow with the combined but informal contributions of all by following an irregular course without much order or direction. The main difficulty is that, because so much of contemporary life is on the run, few conversations allow enough time for the organized telling of happenings. Still, even small conversations furnish a basis for developing narrative skills, and of course conversational skills themselves.

The Importance of Mealtimes

Mealtimes are perhaps the best occasions for developing something more than hit and run exchanges. Unfortunately, for many one- and two-parent working families this too often means a hasty sandwich or snack before rushing off for the evening, with the parent(s) eating at separate times. Worse, infants and young children are frequently fed separately by one of the parents or a nanny, with the parent(s) then eating later. The children cannot experience mealtime conversation in any depth. Conversing with adults during mealtime is an important basis for the development of communication skills and successful participation in the abstract verbal tasks of schoolroom activities, as research has repeatedly shown.

PHOTO BY RON WOOD

Figure 9-6. Mealtimes in Day Care Are Opportune Situations to Encourage Conversations to Develop Theme and Social Skills

The first thing to do then is arrange a family schedule that calls for all members of the family to eat together in a sit-down meal at least a few nights each week, whether the home includes only a single parent and child, or a large extended family. This practice needs to be established soon after the period the infant begins to partake of solid foods. Parents will find that infants will acquire organized self-feeding skills more rapidly in the context of adult models they can imitate. Inclusion in the family group will also temper the oppositional tendencies between parents and children, but above all it is an excellent setting for acquiring language at all stages of development. (See Chapter 5 on activities for talking with infants.)

Encouraging Participation

Infants' first participation will consist largely of having the adults (and older children) label or talk about food items and eating, but over the course of their second year, as infants start to make phrases, adults can begin to address occasional comments about the day's incidents to the infant. In highly communicative families, infants are likely to make their own contributions to the flow of conversation, expanding the scope of what they say as their sentence construction powers expand. In any case, to foster children's participation, enjoyment, and conversational development, it is important to balance the proportions of time devoted to topics according to their interest among all the family members, and to show interest in each participant's contribution, no matter how limited. Hearing about the complexities and abstractions of the adults' concerns and experiences is stimulating and even interesting to children, despite their limited comprehension, if the talk is occasionally phrased simply and clearly and the children are guaranteed a regular airing of their own concerns and experiences. Cooperation and fair play are the keys to harmony.

Conversations in Large Families and Day Care Groups

In large families and day care settings, relations can be difficult, competitive and even chaotic, but the main thing is to ensure that no child gets lost in the round of talk. This will necessitate continual alertness by the adults, mediating among the parties, seeing that the older, and highly verbal children (or adults) do not cast the little ones into the shadows or into the role of clown who acts out physically to get the attention her or his budding language skills do not seem to allow. Tempering the pace of conversation will also help. Successful conversations, in other words, require a degree of leadership control by older members. One need not adhere rigidly to parliamentarian practices (i.e., *Roberts Rules of Order*), but to work well someone has to ensure some balance between spontaneity and order to ensure all get their turn and feel included, regardless of skill level.

Discussions

The rules and settings for discussions are not substantially different from those used in an orderly conversation, even though the purpose of a discussion may involve a formal goal, such as to resolve someone's problem at school or work or to develop understanding of some concept or issue, such as how to cooperate or the distribution of chores in the home. Obviously, young children must be engaged at their level of understanding, but the rules for taking turns and ensuring participation and fair play are much the same. The principal difference is that because there is a specific topic and goal involved, more structure and less spontaneity is necessary to ensure that the flow of comments follow a course related to the topic and problem to be solved, if there is one.

VIDEO PHOTO BY MICHAEL MAJOROS

Figure 9-7. Even Verbal Two-Year-Olds Can Be Engaged in Quite Serious Discussions

For the early years, one does not expect lengthy and profound discussions, of course. Interest and verbal competence will develop gradually through choosing topics and relating discussion elements to the children's activities and the familiar world of home, day care, neighborhood, and the immediate environment. New and more general ideas can be brought in gradually, making comparisons with the activities children are familiar with, such as talking about the cold of Antarctica in terms of how it feels in winter (when appropriate) or the speed of rockets by how a stone travels when thrown. Discussions lasting no more than 3 or 4 minutes are about right for the infant who is just mastering the use of sentences and around 10 or 15 minutes for the youngster whose narrative powers are rapidly taking shape. The issues and problems concerned would also necessarily be quite concrete and related to the children's daily experiences. Issues about small duties, discussions of plans for the afternoon, a weekend or an outing, and relations between siblings or playmates are reasonable areas to address.

Discussions, planned or unplanned, can be held at any time, including mealtimes. It helps to conduct discussions in settings that the problems relate to, however. For example, sit in the playroom for a discussion concerning a question of putting away toys. This is obviously essential in approaching rudimentary science concepts, such as holding discussions about floating or how boats move in a sink or bathtub. Timing a discussion to follow on the heels of an incident related to the problem is also essential, such as an incident of one sibling hoarding the toys or hitting the other.

Verbal analysis should not be expected to solve all social problems and is no substitute for the mediation of day-to-day relations and activities by parents and other caregivers. Discussions nevertheless raise consciousness and help the child grasp the nature of the problems and issues involved. They also give direction and techniques in his or her efforts in daily living and in understanding scientific concepts. The competencies in language acquired through conversation and discussion are vital tools for expanding children's social and cognitive skills.

Sociodramatic Play

This arena for developing language competence through theme activity grows out of the sociodramatic play children begin to engage in as early as the end of their first year, at first alone and then gradually in groups. The first steps in this direction start with children imitating bits and pieces of adult actions in the routines of eating, dressing, household chores, and other everyday activities. Gradually the child moves from no more than holding a spoon to a doll's mouth to carrying out an extended series of simulated tasks, such as preparing cereal, serving it in dishes, setting the table, sitting down at the table, eating, clearing the table, and cleaning and washing up.

The Importance of Language in Social Play

Typically, language is an important agent of social play from the beginning. It serves to guide and coordinate what children do, and expands in importance parallel with the development of social skills. By the ages of three to four they are often capable of coordinating a variety of activities in a complex social scene involving several children playing social and occupational roles of different family members, teachers, and friends. Language is an integral and extended part of the process: the players give one another task instructions and reflect on one another's life styles, daily practices, and special doings, in a kind of parody of adult gossip. Other than providing ample opportunities for sociodramatic play, is there any need to think about organizing special dramatic play activities to further theme skill development?

Guiding Sociodramatic Play

In general, the richer the infant's language and social experience, the more elaborate and imaginative his/her sociodramatic play. There is also much that can be done to enrich and develop theme organizing skills as they play. Even in the early stages, suggestions about whom to feed what and with what utensils broaden the infant's consciousness of task dimensions and social roles. Modeling additional things to say in a given situation will also help. Proposing related tasks to bring into the play (e.g., cooking cereal, cutting bananas) or new tasks altogether (e.g, picking food items in a store, dressing, fixing a broken pipe) further expand the infant's skills and awareness. Much also depends on seeing that infants have plenty of chances to observe a wide range of real life adult activities from week to week.

As children learn to play together in groups of several children, carrying out a variety of ongoing activities in complicated roles (age 3 on), they become open to guidance in an increasing variety of social and occupational roles and theme activities. They can be helped to develop elaborate schemes of play on such themes as running and traveling on railroads, airplanes, ships, buses, and subways. More involved occupational roles, such as running a store, will involve performing all the different worker and consumer personnel roles that the children can create.

Occupational Role Play: Steering Around Stereotypes

Too often occupational theme play in the nursery school, day care, or home is restricted to the activities of stereotypic male-dominated firemen and postmen, or playing doctor with boys as the doctor and girls as the nurse. Substituting terms such as *fire workers* and *letter carriers* is a start toward broadening the activities, but encouraging children of both sexes into the various roles and tasks and expanding the number of occupations used in play are even more important. Setting up reasonable facsimiles of environments for office workers (desks, typewriters, computers, copiers, etc.), for blue collar (plumbing, carpentry, electrical and other trades), and for occupations in transportation, store, and factory settings, will greatly extend the interests and skills of both boys and girls. Paint contours of desks, computers, stoves, store counters, and similar figures on cardboard cartoons to represent different props. Broadening the choices of things to

PHOTO BY SARAH PUTNAM

Figure 9-8. Starting Children Early with Cross-Gender Activities, Such as Encouraging Boys to Play with Dolls and Furniture, Will Do Much to Break Down Gender Stereotyping

do and roles to play serves to buck the traditional social pressures to lock boys into exclusively mechanical things and girls into dolls and household activities.

However, making diverse props freely available and offering suggestions to get different forms of occupational play started will not by themselves prevent children from sometimes pushing each gender into certain occupations ("boys can't be nurses or secretaries" and "girls can't be pilots or bosses"). It is usually necessary not only to suggest particular boys for stereotypical girls roles and vice versa, but also to keep the play going by making further suggestions for what the workers do in the unaccustomed role tasks. Certain children are likely to resist the changes more than others and, ultimately, unless cross-gender sociodramatic play experiences are reinforced by related experiences from other sources in the children's daily lives, they may be difficult to pursue with any consistency. It thus becomes quite important to coordinate these efforts in dramatic play with efforts to involve both boys and girls in non-gender traditional forms of household activity and to expose them to similar stories and information books, as discussed earlier. Fortunately, the diverse occupations of many working mothers today and the wider participation of fathers in domestic chores are both likely to make so-called cross-gender play activities more viable.

To be successful, any suggestions you make must tune into the child's current interests and level of understanding. Try to steer a course between stimulation and intrusion, developing the children's role play skills and broadening their interests gradually. The problem is no different from the one of trying to use balanced styles of interaction with children in stimulating language under any other circumstances. The goal is to guide by occasional, well-timed suggestions that encourage the full play of children's energies and initiatives to develop themes on their own, being careful not to disrupt or dominate the ongoing process.

Organized Dramatic Skits

Toward the end of the preschool years or the beginning of the elementary school years, children sometimes become interested in organized dramatic forms and engage in assigned roles following written scripts. The new activity requires performing a set role in relation to other players' defined roles that follow the development of an organized story line. In a sense they will already have had practice in coordinating their actions and motivations in this way. But because sociodramatic play has no

---

Box 32
A Parent Guide to Sociodramatic Play

First, *talk about plans for a play corner* with your children and involve them in the following steps to get the activities going on a regular basis.

Second, *collect a variety of props* selected to represent several occupational themes and family activities. These would include:

Clothes: Jeans, heavy shoes, and worker's caps for blue collar/ factory work; business jacket, shirt, and tie for office jobs. Old clothes, even if they don't fit, work very well.

Tools: Miscellaneous tools suitable to suggest various trades, such as pliers, screwdriver for blue collar, and pencils, paper, and toy telephone for office occupations.

Equipment: A few large toy square and rectangular building blocks (around 1' square and 1' x 18") will serve as work-benches, office desks, machines and almost any other type of equipment. Empty cardboard packing cartons also lend themselves to many uses.

Third, *look for a suitable corner* of some room, close to the site of common family activities, but out of the way of traffic, where props can be stored and readily used for play and children can be readily encouraged.

Fourth, *arrange props in categories on shelves* placed in the play corner, so as to be visibly and physically accessible on demand. Three or four boards placed in tiers on bricks at either end can be put together in various ways.

---

formally structured sequence, the children's actions and motivations are able to develop very loosely by following their spontaneous inclinations and whatever suggestions adults might have introduced in orchestrating their play. Organizing children's informal play into formal dramatic

Box 32 (cont.)

Fifth, *plan convenient times to encourage dramatic play and try to arrange for a suitable playmate* or two from time to time (depending on the number of suitable playmates in your own family), ones you know are likely to enjoy and contribute imaginatively to the play.

Sixth, *encourage your children to play* with the materials at any convenient time, making suggestions in terms of different social role activity and occupational themes, as necessary to get the play going. Talk for example about repairing a furnace, making a car in a factory, preparing a meal, working a computer, repairing a telephone pole line, selling shoes in a store, writing office memos, mentioning a few specifics of what the activities actually entail.

Seventh, *find books that tell about various occupations* and read them to your child during the week or so you try to encourage play around a particular occupational theme.

Eighth, *schedule a visit or two with your child to a site* where he/she can observe the activities of workers in the theme occupation you are encouraging in the play and reading about in books.

Ninth, don't forget to *encourage both boys and girls to play all of the occupational and household activity roles.*

Tenth, try to develop cross-cultural themes occasionally. Many children between 18 months and 5 years of age will spontaneously engage in some sort of social play as soon as the props are brought out, even before they are placed in the play corner. However, *a little imaginative input from adults* now and then will greatly enrich the quality and frequency of the play and the development of language-involved theme activity.

pieces, on the other hand, will lead them towards a more conceptual and self-controlled mastery of themes. In the same way books demand attention to thought and abstract themes, acting in plays may demand playing and interrelating roles in more complex themes and plot lines than

those that usually emerge in the informal way young children spontaneously imagine and orchestrate their sociodramatic play.

As usual, start slowly, perhaps gathering no more than two or three
children to play parts in short one-act skits lasting a few minutes or so.
One-act plays are likely to be a staple form for some years, although
children with more sociodramatic play experience and well-developed
verbal and cognitive skills can manage longer pieces of two or three short
acts. Themes related to concerns about their daily life have the most
appeal. Skits about peer conflicts in and out of school, about school
learning problems, and about problems of family life will work well. But
the appeal will also vary with dramatic quality, simplicity and directness
of the language, ideas and characterizations, and clarity of the plot line.
Dramatizations using animal figures and fairy tale creatures have long
had special appeal, as the abundance of such figures in children's books
and on television testifies. The possibility of using or adapting selected
adult plays by the pre-teen years should not be overlooked, provided they
are not too complex or loaded with violence or threatening themes, and
are presented in ways that touch the children's own lives.

Arranging Social Play Time

It must be asked how much effort busy parents can be expected to devote
to guiding their children in sociodramatic play activities at home. In group
day care, sociodramatic play is a mainstay of daily activity, although the
quality varies from center to center. A good center is one where the staff
frequently rearranges settings, ensures that a wide range of occupational
and other play materials are available, and has at least one teacher always
on tap to furnish regularly well-timed suggestions for diversifying themes
and find ways to involve social isolates.

Dramatic play in the home, informally or formally with written plays,
is equally helpful for children, but the necessary groups are not always
easily arranged, nor is the time and skill always available for the kind of
attention it needs. Not many families and children can or will want to
devote the serious efforts over many years that it may take to develop a
deep interest in acting. Yet children's social insights, competence in
language, and appreciation of literature will certainly improve according
to the quality and frequency of sociodramatic play and acting in plays.
What can parents do?

One should start with the realization that one cannot do everything,
and that priorities need to be established as to what is important and

possible. Certainly family values count most. Activities such as telling stories and drawing may be more important to many families than skills in role playing. For those families who are interested, however, there are certain practical arrangements that will help without having to invest all one's energies in the development of social and dramatic play skills. One way is to collect a variety of clothes, tools, and equipment that will serve as props for the many possible social and occupational roles young children could play. These props need not be fancy or extensive. Inexpensive worker hats and coveralls or jeans, real or toy wrenches, some pipes, bits of wire, real or toy hammers and saws, nails, and the like, together with an all-purpose crude wooden bench or table and a few gadgets to simulate manufacturing machines will do very well for various trades and factory settings. Be sure to supervise activities with such potentially dangerous tools closely. A few empty cans and cartons, paper, and a simple calculator with the same bench will work for a store, and an old typewriter and tables, together with paper and cartons to simulate copiers will do for an office environment, along with old ties and jackets to suggest formal atmosphere. A second aid is to set aside a special room or corner for storing these materials in easily accessible ways to encourage frequent use.

A third is to periodically help your child or children set up and develop a social role play project. Encourage them to bring in one or two playmates for the specific purpose of playing in a project of this sort, and set aside blocks of time once or twice a week if possible (for yourself or for whoever cares for the child) to supervise and guide the play in the manner described above. Encouraging the playmates' families to set up similar environments and take turns in planning occasions for social role play will reinforce interest and expand opportunities for development. Setting up formal skits or plays with scripts is of course likely to be more the province of those families with specialized interests, whether professional or amateur. Finding and adapting scripts, memorizing lines and formally rehearsing, staging, and performing the plays become major issues in formal drama, however informally projected and small the audiences.

Telling Stories

Telling a story can be a natural extension of story reading or it can grow out of the practice of narrating the ordinary events of the moment. If, as is often the case, children ask for a certain book to be read again and again, they may begin to relate what will happen on the next page before you do, or they may begin to talk about the story events after the reading. Sometimes, when a story is repeated often enough, they like to go through the whole story in this way, until they reach a point where they ask you to tell the story without the book. Then they will also usually comment on certain climaxes, like "Did she find the lost doggy?" or "Then he reached the top of the mountain." Sooner or later the children themselves may be telling whole sections and eventually the entire tale, often selecting and embellishing what appeals to them.

Encouraging Storytelling or Reading Skills

Of course, few children actually become real story tellers. When they do, it is probably because of the quality of encouragement they have received, which suggests that all children can develop some skills in this direction. Repeatedly reading favorite books is one of the obvious bases for encouraging storytelling, but storytelling skills aren't likely to develop unless adults use an interactive style that encourages the child's repeated participation in the process of unfolding the tale. Another factor is how much adults tell about the events in their own words, rather than adhering literally to the text. The difference is often a matter of taste, yet the different styles may have different consequences. Sticking to text in a repeatedly read book may lead the child to become curious about learning to read words and phrases, while telling and retelling in one's own words

PHOTO BY JACQUELINE PAUL

Figure 9-9. *Reading Books Can Lead to an Interest in Reading or Telling Stories*

Box 33
Two Avenues to Storytelling

Through Listening to Story Books
Read to the child frequently.

Continue to tell the stories in your own words, rather than sticking to the text, even long after the child can follow text.

Interact with the child: Pause from time to time and ask questions to encourage the child to tell the story; ask about
What is happening (in a picture)
What is going to happen next
What happened that led to what is happening now

Develop an interest in a favorite book by reading it many times, engaging the child in telling more and more of the story him/herself.

Note. Telling the stories is more likely to lead to an interest in story-telling, while reading text is more likely to lead to an interest in learning to read.

Through Example
Tell stories yourself, either making up stories or retelling stories from books.

Tell about ordinary happenings in a storylike way: Tell the events in order, pointing up incidents dramatically in terms of their contribution toward the outcome, leaving the final outcome as a surprise.

Encourage other family members/day care staff to tell stories or talk about their everyday experiences in the same way.

Engage the child in helping with parts of the story from time-to-time, asking questions about what will happen next.

Encourage the child to tell stories as he or she develops, or about his or her ordinary experiences. (See also Box 30, Telling about Experiences.)

Set up informal *storytelling times* with family members and friends/day care staff, inviting especially those known to be good story-tellers, and include children as both audience and participants.

is more likely to elicit storytelling behavior in the child.

Actually, telling stories to children and reading books to them need not result in conflicting courses of development, but the different styles they demand make it less likely for children to become skilled in both spheres. Storytelling depends much on personal style, on the way words are chosen and themes are developed. On the other hand, reading anchors the performance to a text whose words and themes are prepared in advance, allowing less leeway for personal expression, except in discussing the text. Hearing stories told may also be less essential for later development than hearing stories read: the former leads to the fading world of oral literature, while the latter is an important basis for learning to read, which is indispensable for school learning and coping in our complex world, as well as for the enjoyment of literature and aesthetic development.

In many ways, telling stories is more akin to writing stories than to reading them. The actual telling of stories is far more complex than either telling a story from a book, which is essentially a retelling, or telling about a personal experience or an observed event, both of which are also a kind of retelling. Telling and writing original stories are both creative, complex mental processes, demanding that the author draw from her or his imagination different threads of experience and put them together into an organized and sequential whole. But because telling stories uses oral language with patterns of intonation and other cues that face-to-face communication provides, and does not require the added strict rules needed for translating oral language into written forms, it is less formal and abstract than writing stories.

Routes to Developing Story Telling Skills

Adults who tend to read stories in their own words are also more likely to be people who like to tell stories of their own. Telling stories rather than reading them sets an example for children to follow, of course, but they may not follow unless they are involved in the storytelling process themselves. Simply telling story after story will undoubtedly stimulate the child's imagination, but passive listening does not offer the kind of practice that may be necessary for the active, creative role of conceptualizing and verbally organizing a set of events into a theme-centered narrative.

When a child begins telling stories out of the experience of telling about ordinary events, it is usually because some caregiver has set an example by weaving common experiences into stories. The adult tells about a happening in an imaginative way, selecting and highlighting details to construct an organized dramatic sequence, and introducing motivations and conflict between the actors and the events. The adult may also ask children questions to help them see potential story qualities in everyday experiences and to begin to reconstruct ordinary events in dramatic form.

Whatever route is followed to encourage storytelling, it helps to establish a comfortable, relaxed setting to allow time for the imagination to reflect and rework events. Practicing storytelling before small audiences of peers is also invaluable for encouraging children to perform and develop. Later on in their development, larger audiences may inspire certain children to take special delight in the process and to work more and more to improve their skills. They may enjoy enchanting people by assuming the important cultural role of story teller.

Poetry and Singing

Poetry and singing are two complementary activities, because both involve stress on rhythm and meter and both attempt to convey experience thematically in a more evanescent, less expositional form than prose. Poetry presents images and metaphors to express personal ideas and feelings about life that touch chords in others relating to their own experiences in the world. It ranges in form from the highly formal, classical, 12-syllable Alexandrine verse to the freely flowing reflections and imagery of most contemporary verse.

Music

Music also takes many forms, with and without words, from the simple pentatonic scales with reed pipes and flutes to the eight-note scales of classical European music, the syncopations and beat of jazz and rock, and the modern atonal forms. Music enjoys the added power of tone and melody whose intrinsic appeal makes the development of appreciation and skill easier than with poetry. But this may be largely because poetry is less prominent than music in American life in general and in child-rearing practices in particular. Children's interest in both music and poetry grow most easily out of the experiences of social interaction play with verse and song long used with babies in relation to physical play. The discussion here will center on poetry. Musical development is a topic for another book.

Social Play with Verse

Because many of the early verse experiences of babies are rooted in social play with adults, the appreciation of poetry develops through oral expression, the natural form in which poetry is meant to be communicated. In social play, adults recite verse as they touch or play with the child physically; the verse is recited without the stilted quality that is sometimes difficult to avoid in reading poetry. (See Chapter 5, Where to Talk with Infants for more details.)

Developing Appreciation For Poetry

Development of poetry appreciation in infants is a matter of gradually expanding the length of the verses you recite to them (see Box 12, Social Play with Verse and Song), as well as increasing the diversity and complexity of themes you choose, as infants widen their understanding and begin speaking themselves. By the time they reach the stage of putting words together into sentences (anywhere from 12 months on), they will respond eagerly and attentively to verses of 3 or 4 or more lines, and over the course of a few months or so, they will come to enjoy lively verse recitations of as many as 8 to 10 lines or more. As their capacity for listening to longer verses expands, the recitations no longer need be accompanied by the physical play that is common to the beginning social play with simple one, two- or three-line verses.

As infants develop they nevertheless continue to appreciate mainly themes that relate to their own experiences. They can dispense with the physical play and dramatizations because their growing language skills enable them to hold things in mind more easily. But this increasing ability to understand the abstractions of language comes slowly to embrace the hopes, fears, and psychological perspectives of adults and older children. What they do respond to about the adult world are the descriptions of simple, direct actions, the movements of people doing things and having things happen to them physically, things similar to what they understand out of their own experience or from what they see and can imagine. Hence the appeal of Mother Goose, in which actions are concretely described, if sometimes on seemingly ridiculous themes, such as:

> There was an old woman who lived in a shoe
> Who had so many children she didn't know what to do.
>   or
> Humpty Dumpty sat on a wall.

Humpty Dumpty had a great fall.

In the same way, metaphors (symbolic comparisons) based on subtleties of meaning and mood reflections ("It was a blue day") or dreams of glory ("The sky opened out for Terry") do not come quickly. On the other hand, the actions of animals are a kind of concrete metaphor that children grasp very early, as long as the animals' experiences and adventures are rooted in physical activities and well-defined obstacles.

Children can also respond with increasing sensitivity to the rhythm, meter, rhyming, and other poetic qualities of the verse. Their readiness depends on the range of their experiences in hearing the play of language sound patterns in verse and related activities (see Box 26, Strategies for Nonsense Word Play). But their response also depends on the expressive skill and style of the person who recites the verses. The traditional lore of Mother Goose Nursery rhymes, in particular, gather together many ancient folk ideas and experiences from pre-industrial rural life that have little meaning for the child of our day. For example, "Ring around the Rosies/ Pocket full of Posies/ We all fall down" refers to the time of the great plagues that swept Europe; people carried charms of flowers to ward off the disease, but often died ("fall down") anyway. Yet their catchy rhythms that present people, animals and events in often zany but concrete ways, such as *Jack and Jill*, *Little Jack Horner*, and dozens of other verses, are easy to recite, and continue to capture the attention of young children, generation after generation.

Simplicity and clarity of expression in saying the verse, with an emphasis on conveying meaning, generally work best. Pyrotechnics and melodramatic exaggerations if relied on too much tend to undercut the intrinsic values of the verse and hamper development of poetic appreciation. Most important is to recite verses frequently and to advance the complexity of the material as the child's understanding grows, going over the old favorites many times before rushing too fast to new and sophisticated ones.

Reading Poetry

Yet those who feel self-conscious about reciting, even in the intimacy of family and friends, or those who cannot take the time to learn verses by heart, will nevertheless transmit much of value to children through reading verses. The meaning conveyed by the sound is projected through reading aloud, even if not with the same spontaneity and fullness of expression that live recitation can communicate. It is probably also true that some adults read with more life than they do when they recite. Fortunately, verses read many times are often retained by children, as much as if they were recited. This is no idle goal, for verses learned are verses available to arouse and recapture the poetic experience at times when the written versions are not immediately available, on walks in the country and around the hearth or in friendly gatherings illuminated by all the richness that poetry can convey.

As understanding and appreciation develop, there is no need to restrict offerings to nursery rhymes and children's verse. By the late preschool years, children will begin to enjoy adult poetry that is laced with concrete imagery they can connect with their own lives, if it is introduced in fragments and repeated a number of times. Actually, certain contemporary poetry for children is in fact more complex than children's verse of time past. On the other hand, the fluid, concrete imagery employed successfully in certain adult verse bridges the worlds of adulthood and childhood, reaching people across all ages, as, in some senses, all of the best poetry for children does.

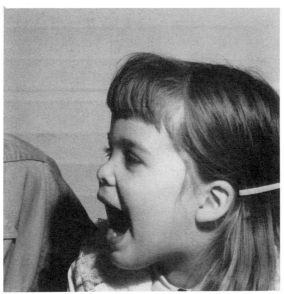

PHOTO BY JACQUELINE PAUL

Figure 9-10. Repeated Poetry Reading Will Often Lead To Spontaneous Recitation

Chapter 10

Starting Late: Correcting Language Delay

WHAT IS LANGUAGE DELAY? THE MEANING OF FALLING BEHIND

When children fail to talk on schedule, it often means they have not enjoyed the kind of language experiences the local culture practices. In the rural farm settings and tribal folk life of past eras, language was not the central requirement for coping with the concrete tasks of cultivation that dominated daily life. But in our world of endless communication demands, falling behind the cultural norms of language development can be serious. Children who have less language experience than the contemporary culture prescribes may well fail to reach the usual benchmarks of saying real words by a year or so, or beginning to combine words into sentences before age two. Poorly stimulated children may know and speak only a few words by age two or even three. How far behind a child lags will depend on two things: (1) the age the child has reached when a decision is made to pay more attention to language, and (2) the quality of the language experienced up until that age.

Not Detecting Speech Lags

The effects of language delay are frequently not apparent during infancy, particularly among parents out of touch with issues of child rearing, and sometimes among caregivers in family day care or in poorly organized group care programs. Parents, especially busy working parents, who fail to monitor their child's nanny or day care program, or seldom share observations on their children's development with members of the extended family or other parents—all common trends in the high pressure rootless communities of our era—may not notice any delay until it reaches large proportions. Day care staff may lack adequate training in child development, or centers may be plagued with high turnover (of staff or children), program disorganization, or other problems that result in lax monitoring of each child's development.

Nagging doubts of harried parents or day care staff are sometimes comforted by expectations of children later catching up, once they get past a lagging stage, or by plans to find a later time to devote more attention to the child. There is also a certain amount of leeway in rates of progress at different stages. Delays in understanding or saying words, for example, can often be compensated for by sudden advances at later points in response to new experiences and insights.

Temporary Delays

Most successful catch-ups or reversals of language delay, however, are likely to be confined to children whose slowdowns are temporary rather than the result of long term developmental effects of under-stimulation or stress accumulating from early infancy. Temporary setbacks are common in even the best home and day care language environments. Families move or experience reversals such as job losses, accidents, illness, deaths, and increased parental work demands, all of which usually produce disruptions and tensions that threaten the quality of infant care and learning.

Delays In Our Research

In our research studies (see complete section on research programs in Appendix), one 8-month-old who had begun to say words stopped talking when the family moved—until her toys were unpacked. Remodeling the house had the same effect in another family. In still another, parents left their 10-month-old boy, whose vocabulary had reached 20 words, with the grandmother for a 10-day vacation; he became silent for almost three months. Phenobarbital prescribed for convulsions arising from a high fever slowed and slurred the speech of a boy who had just started saying phrases. Another boy who had also begun constructing phrases ceased for two months just after his first birthday, when his mother broke her nose, his father was hospitalized for a knee operation, and everyone in the family got the flu, one after the other.

Disruptions in day care can have similar effects. Staff turnover, illness, conflict and personal problems, or the transfer of an infant to a new teacher or group, can easily result in short-term language (and other) delays or emotional problems that hamper development. Attention to language and other learning slows, schedules become ragged, or important relations with teachers or peers are altered. In some cases, certain children become favorites, receiving more attention than other quiet or difficult infants, who may become socially isolated.

Usually such reversals are temporary, as they were in all of our family and day care studies. Toys were unpacked, the household settled down, remodeling was completed, parents returned from vacation, illness abated and medicine was terminated, and family life and schedules were resumed. In our day care studies, new teachers usually established constructive relations, teacher conflicts were largely resolved, infants adapted to the new group or peer changes, and changing relations often reduced the effects of favoritism. As research programs, we could make special efforts to advise parents or teachers. But in many cases parent or teacher insight resulted in added attention even before the disruptive problems were solved, because, having seen for themselves the results of high attention to language, they were struck by the effects of the disruptions.

The complexities of child care in day care, however, meant that specially planned arrangements to anticipate problems were useful: Teachers were sometimes each assigned in our research programs to a subset of infants, matched to their own styles, to oversee the infants' week-to-week development, even though all teachers had to tend to the daily care of all children in the group. This minimized the effects of favoritism, isolation, and other problems. We also arranged meetings between individual teachers and parents that produced insights for both parties and renewed development for the child. Encouraging two previously almost mute isolates to play side by side at parallel activities (puzzles) resulted in their developing close relations and a bubbling of language between them that soon extended to relations with adults and other children. In another instance, a well-matched teacher was assigned to an infant whose language was failing to progress because his parents "couldn't stand helpless infants." This 10-month-old boy soon began to thrive because of the caregivers' special efforts, and once he attained a more verbal and autonomous toddler stage, the parents began to accept their child. Thus, early temporary delays can be readily reversed in both the home and day care, given a little insight and effort.

THE DIFFICULTY OF CATCHING UP

There are nevertheless certain limits or constraints on catching up, especially with long-standing delays. A problem of delayed or poor speech development sometimes comes dramatically to parents' attention with the child's first extensive contact with other children, sometimes not until age two or three. Entry to day care or nursery school, or the formation

---

Box 34
Common Histories of Delay and Trying to Catch Up in Children without Hearing Loss or Organic Problems

Early Infancy (Birth to 18 months)
Disposing Conditions
1. Primary caregivers use little or no language in handling infant and seldom talk to anyone else with the child present.
2. Caregiver failure to recognize or realize significance of lack of infant vocalization and progress in word learning.

Common Situations
1. Non-verbal (and frequently depressed) parent(s) who have few opportunities to observe or exchange information with other adults as a result of isolation from their extended family or any parenting community.
2. Single or two-parent families who work long hours and poorly monitor their infant's care in connection with one or more of the following:
   a. A poorly trained or otherwise inadequate, substitute home caregiver.
   b. Poor quality, overcrowded group day care.
   c. Poor quality, non-professional family day care.

Later Infancy (18 to 36 months)
Reinforcing Conditions
1. Blocked awareness by caregiver(s) of significance of child's poor progress in language development, as child falls progressively further behind obvious minimal norms.

of a neighborhood play group are typical occasions. Suddenly the gap between the other children's use of sentences—however simple—and their own child's stumbling use of words, becomes plain enough for parents to see and children to experience. Parents and children alike suddenly have a standard for comparison. The parents may quickly scramble to remedy the situation and the child attempts to cope as best he or she can.

Box 34 (cont.)

2. Child develops gestural, nonverbal modes of communication, increasing sense of failure and awareness of social deviance from other children.
3. Belated sporadic and unsystematic caregiver attempts to make up for lost time in helping child learn to talk, often varying between high pressure and giving up.
4. A cycle of nonproductive interaction may develop between child and primary caregivers that reinforces the child's sense of failure and nonverbal modes of functioning, generates resistance to change and blocks efforts to learn to talk.

Common Situations
1. Form of child care continuing more or less unchanged from one of the early circumstances until late in the period, eventually resulting in relatively more serious forms of delay.
2. Chance contact with other parents, and especially chance observation of other infants advancing at normal rates, or a new home caregiver draws parent attention to difficulty. Parents or new caregiver are unable to change life styles or parent-child interaction styles sufficiently to effect change without special help.
3 Admission of infant to professional or family day care whose staff soon recognizes delay, but child's degree of delay and forms of functioning are too well entrenched for child to acquire language in the normal group environment without special help.
4. Eventual recognition by group or family day care staff of increasingly obvious language delay by the infant compared to their other infants results in unsuccessful efforts to rectify situation because of the lateness of the effort and the continuing general inadequacy of the program.

The parents now find it is not so easy to help their child catch up, however. Pouring words and instructions at the child may build frustration and resistance to talking at all, yet even when parents now try to work calmly and gently their child still seems to fall further and further behind other children of the same age. The gap widens more and more as children progressing well learn the increasingly complex language skills culturally expected of older children, while their child remains stuck at an infantlike level. The parent and soon the child become all too painfully aware of the dilemma.

Delayed children themselves can sense when they are relegated to lesser roles in play and social responsibilities in the daily activities that increasingly depend on language to speak the parts and understand adult instructions during the preschool years. They may be assigned the role of "baby" in domestic play, for example, or simply become onlookers in the complicated sociodramatic activities of occupational role and construction play. And teachers tend to invite other children who understand quickly to take the lead in games or to assist in bringing out the clay and other special toys. How are children to cope when they are incapable of carrying out the roles and tasks expected of them while their schoolmates advance steadily further and further ahead?

What Nonverbal Infants Learn Instead of Speech: Gestures

Children who have failed to understand and use words and sentences according to the schedule their fellow infants follow are often not simply delayed or behind schedule. Typically they have or are beginning to acquire different ways of communicating and solving problems. Chief among these are the use of gestures and a coping mode of "learned helplessness," a kind of resignation and passive expectation that others will anticipate their needs and help them over troublesome problems. Such gestural and passive ways may work quite adequately in the intimacy of the family of a few members who are well acquainted with one another's little idiosyncracies.

But by the time the child reaches the preschool ages of three to five, busy teachers working with numbers of children in day care lack the time to compensate for children's inability to follow along with a group and make their wants known through the quick and direct method of verbal expression. And even if preschool teachers can manage to compensate, the child soon has to face the even more demanding verbal modes of elementary school for which such nonverbal modes are even less suitable. Answering and asking questions, reciting orally and reading—

all totally dependent on language, initiative and independence in carrying on school work—simply do not work with physical gestures and passive dependence.

Alternative modes can also take the form of constant, wound up physical activity, better known as hyperactive behavior. While not necessarily associated with language delay, supercharged physical activity with the child continually on the move, skipping superficially from task to task, can be extremely disruptive to the child's development and to the caregiver's patience.

Degrees of Delay Originating in Poor Language Experiences

How does a parent go about encouraging speech in a child at a later age? Remember that this is a child whose development has not been reaching full potential according to the developmental time table outlined in Box 2, Chapter 2. Let us look at various degrees and types of delay and what to do about them. *The focus here will be on slightly to moderately delayed children who have no apparent physical or organic mental basis for their slowness in learning to talk.* This means children who have experienced poor or inadequate attention to language in the home or day care during infancy. The delay may be as slight as failing to say any words until 15 months (instead of 12 months) or not relating experiences until age 3 1/2 (instead of 3), to as much as only beginning to use words at age two (instead of 1) or not being able to tell about their experiences until 4 1/2 or more (instead of the normal 3). A schedule of the degrees of slight and moderate delay for certain major developmental achievements in language is displayed in Box 35. (These delays are of course even further behind developmental norms for children reared in enriched language environments. See Box 2.)

By definition, any delay in language development beyond the age ranges indicated for moderate delay would be considered more extreme, possibly requiring professional help beyond the kind of activities discussed in the following section. In this discussion I will not take up in detail questions of extreme forms of delay, such as lack of any speech past age 2 1/2 or persistent stuttering, which are problems arising from long neglect, serious emotional or organically based problems. Yet any definitions of delay are in some sense arbitrary and even serious delays and problems can sometimes be remedied with relatively simple measures. It is helpful to assume an optimistic stance and to know that most delays take specific forms that can be remedied without heroic efforts or extensive professional help.

Box 35
Benchmarks of speech Delay

Schedule of Slight and Moderate Delays in Speech Development at Different Stages of Development

Stage[a]	Steps	Age Ranges of Acquisition (Months)		
		Norms	Slight Delay	Moderate Delay
Words	First real words (3)	11-12	13-15	16-18
	10-20 word vocabulary	18-20	21-24	25-28
Phrases/	Two-word combinations	18-20	21-24	25-28
Sentences	Three-word phrases	22-24	25-29	30-34
	Talks in sentences	24-27	28-33	34-39
Themes	Relates experiences	33-36	36-41	42-47
	Uses basic rules of grammar	48	49-55	56-62

[a] Because of their relative independence from word, sentence, and theme development, pronunciation errors are not listed.

NB- Note that the length of delays increases slightly with the stage because delays at later stages reflect an accumulation of difficulties from earlier stages. Norms drawn from sources listed in Box 2. Delays are empirically defined.

SHIFTING LANGUAGE DELAYED TODDLERS AND PRESCHOOLERS FROM GESTURAL TO VERBAL MODES OF COMMUNICATION

Parents or day care teachers who begin to notice lags in speech development need to encourage the child to talk and understand instructions through words, rather than gestures, and to avoid anticipating their child's wants and solving the child's problems on the basis of gestural requests. Here are a few principles that may help to alter these dead end modes of functioning. They are not, however, a panacea, and must be used with caution and common sense.

1. Respond to even the slightest effort the child makes to say something by acceding to the apparent request or agreeing with the apparent observation. Answer the request in words, as well as in deed (e.g., say "Here's a glass of juice," as you hand it to the child), and frame

---

Box 36
Shifting from Gestural to Verbal Modes of Communication: Behavioral Principles

1. Respond positively to any efforts, however slight, the child makes to communicate his/her wants verbally, always responding in words, repeating what he/she is apparently trying to say, and granting any reasonable request with pleasure and warmth.

2. Any time the child utters a sentence, phrase, word, or even merely vocalizes sounds that could be interpreted as an effort to say something, use the situation to encourage a verbal dialogue, expanding on the child's expression in a complete sentence focused on the apparent topic (e.g., say "Yes, that's a horse," when the child hisses "sss" and points to a picture of a horse).

3. Whenever possible, avoid responding to all requests where the child attempts to communicate solely with gestures. Simply ignore requests where no vocalization is involved.

4. Avoid all confrontations and above all avoid repeated efforts to request the child to answer or say or ask for something in words. In other words, reward spontaneous efforts but don't push and don't punish failures, except in the form of lack of attention.

5. Engage all family members, including older siblings, along with teachers and others having frequent contact with the child in employing the same strategy as much as feasible. Coordinate strategies of day care and home.

the answer into a complete, simple sentence as a model for the child to learn by. If you expand on the child's one-word verbal request (e.g., juice) by saying, "Would you (or, you would) like some juice," be careful of your tone. Say it in a matter-of-fact, friendly way; be sure the child does not feel put down or criticized. Greet all efforts with expressions of obvious (but not anxious or hysterical) pleasure and continued attention.

2. The child's one-word comments about an event (e.g., *doggy*), uttered when seeing a dog jump over a fence, for example, can serve as the basis for the beginnings of simple dialogue, learning to use language as a communication tool. Respond with interest and make a complete sentence, as an example, but stress the key action, *jump*, as well as the term *dog*, saying for example, "Yes, look at the *dog jump* over the fence!" In this way the child gets an example of a key concrete action, which because it has just been so vividly illustrated, is a word likely to stick with the child. Even if the child does not immediately repeat the word *jump*, now is a good moment to provide another example, by making a *jump* and saying something like, "Look at me!" Many children will then spontaneously imitate the adult action, but if your child doesn't, encourage by suggesting, "Let's see you jump," or "Would you like to jump?" The child may repeat the word *jump* at some point (over a series of sessions), but in any case, linking the new word several times to a series of jumping actions will have provided a good session on word learning that can be carried over to other occasions.

3. Avoid or minimize responding to children's requests or demands for attention when they make no effort to use words. When they ask only by pointing to something (e.g., a toy on a high shelf, something in the refrigerator), pay no attention, or ask, "What is it you want? *Tell* me, so I can understand, and get it for you." If they still make no effort to say the name of the thing, turn away or better, say, "I can't help you unless you *tell* me, so I can understand." Be sure not to sound punitive or critical in any way. Be friendly and patient. If the child still says nothing after your second request, it is best to go about doing your activities, to avoid undue pressure on the child, which will only build further resistance.

4. Avoid strong confrontations in the form of insistent and repeated efforts to get the child to say something. Using the dramatic or "teachable moment," as John Dewey used to say, to elicit speech is invaluable, but only if handled spontaneously and lightly. Persistent, direct efforts to instruct a delayed child to talk will usually only lead to frustration and a sense of failure for both parent or teacher and child. Children become more convinced they *can't* talk and parents that the children *won't* talk, both digging in their heels into an unprofitable deadlock.

Teaching Language or Rewarding Spontaneous Speech

The best methods for helping delayed children to master speech, however, may be much the same as those recommended for any child during infancy. These consist of the kind of interactive play with sounds, words, sentences, and themes that advance language development described in Chapters 6 through 9. This may be defined as a strategy of *cognitive developmental stimulation.*

The *common remedial strategy*, the principles of which I have just summarized, is founded on a fundamentally different theory than those described elsewhere throughout the book. The distinction rests on where and how the focus of the effort is to be applied. Remediation *concentrates on the spontaneous communications of children with others in daily activity*. The caregiver's task is one of attempting to shift the child from nonverbal to verbal modes of communication by encouraging and rewarding efforts to talk and ignoring (not responding to) the child's use of nonverbal modes. Such a strategy is governed by behaviorist principles of learning by altering the consequences of the child's behavior through regulating the rewards and punishments incurred. Punishment in this situation consists of the lack of adult attention to nonverbal modes. There is no "curriculum plan," or a program of language to help the child master the rules of language. Rather the strategy is one of trying to take advantage of whatever the child happens to do and use it as a basis to teach language.

A *cognitive developmental strategy* of stimulation, in contrast, focuses on structuring new situations that may give the child planned experiences with language which will furnish information the child is assumed to lack. Because language delayed children fail to use language in ways and at levels culturally expected for their age, the problem is viewed as one of providing them with plenty of new examples of the different language forms and rules they are assumed to be deficient in. In effect one "teaches" the rules of language through labeling and manipulating. In other words, give the child repeated examples of the various rules through interactive language play in ways that are essentially similar to the way you would with a pre-verbal infant.

There are of course certain modifications of the strategy needed when it is used with language delayed infants and preschoolers. These have to do with what the child already knows and does with language, and whether serious emotional problems or extreme forms of language difficulties have incurred. The first question requires some sort of diagnosis (see below). The others may require consultation and treatment with a trained therapist or speech therapist. It is encouraging to note, however, that most problems are not serious enough to prevent language delayed children from enjoying the language play and beginning to speak well with reasonable fluency.

Disadvantages of Behavioral Strategies

While using remedial behavioral principles can certainly help, when used properly, efforts to apply them sometimes make the problem worse. Delays or minor speech difficulties can turn into serious delays and major anxieties over using language.

One root of the problem lies in the difficulty parents and day care teachers face in changing styles. Wholehearted efforts to encourage are haunted by the ghost of past practices. The style a caregiver comes to use with a child is not simply a certain way of doing things. Styles are integral to the ways a caregiver and child are accustomed to interact with each other. Both are used to initiating and responding almost unconsciously in terms of expectations of what the other usually does.

In the case of delayed or deviant speech, it is not only the child who relies on gestures and passive techniques of helplessness for communication to satisfy her or his wants. The caregiver too has come to expect and rely on the child to behave this way. As a result, the caregiver responds automatically in playing the role of responding to these by now ingrained expectations and habits of nonverbal communication. The caregiver does all the reading of nonverbal messages, any talking that occurs, and often most of the actions needed for the child to get what she or he is after.

Such patterns of negative interaction often grow to assume a life of their own, and are difficult to alter or reverse without carefully crafted plans and systematic efforts. It is all too easy for a parent or teacher to lapse into a practice of constant nagging, only barely masked as efforts to reward a child's minimal efforts, a practice that breeds chronic resistance to improvement. Given the long history of relations between parent and child, negative interactions, when they develop, are usually very ingrained and difficult to alter, but such patterns are not uncommon and just about as difficult to reverse even in the professional environment of day care.

Another difficulty lies in the fact that children poor at language often

Box 37
Cognitive Learning Versus Behavioral strategies for Correcting Language Delay

Cognitive Learning   *Behavioral Remediation*

Curriculum Planning

Uses a curriculum plan of language forms sequenced, adapted and, pre-presented at child's current level.

Relies on child's spontaneous expression of language that is often minimal, because of delay.

Focus of Learning Program

Defines learning in terms of mental processes: the child makes inferences about the rules of language from examples provided by skilled speakers, leading to the ability to communicate verbally

Defines learning in terms of behavioral regulation (without regard to cognitive processes and the hierarchy of language rules) to develop language skills

Specific Techniques and Developmental Goals

Combines modeling of examples of language for the child to imitate and infer rules with interpersonal communication and play modes aimed at developing autonomy

Centers on behavioral control modes of reward and punishment (i.e., lack of attention), a contingency-regulated interper-sonal system,which some consider conformity oriented, without systematic (language) content planning

Parenting/Teaching Styles

Furnishing specific techniques to use with planned activities, many of them incorporated into daily routines, helps parents and other familiar caregivers to adapt their previous styles to constructive modes of interactive teaching

Although caregivers are given specific techniques, they often find it difficult to avoid reverting to prior nonproductive styles, such as pushing or scolding, because techniques are to be applied in everyday activities without a plan of language and play activities to use

do not speak enough to reward efforts to talk. *More important, simply praising children's low level efforts does not teach them the rules about language they need to learn.* How can one rely on the accidents of everyday discourse to teach language rules to children whose problem is precisely one of not knowing and using speech adequately? Providing attention and rewards is certainly important, as good relations always are. But without a program of good examples of language for the children to learn from, how can rewards alone help?

For all of these reasons, once a caregiver has discovered that the child is somehow falling behind and needs more help with language and decides to do something about it, the best thing to do is begin using language regularly with the child in constructive ways, taking the initiative to demonstrate the correct forms and rules of language rather than just looking for moments to correct the child's alternative modes of gestural speech and passive anticipation. Though behavioral remedial principles can work in some ways, real progress is likely to come faster and more assuredly from playing many language games with the child in everyday practice. Setting up constructive language activities frequently produces beneficial results, while using remedial techniques (ignoring wrong modes and rewarding desired modes) may yield only marginal results.

Advantages of Cognitive Strategies

Not only does interactive play furnish children with lots of new language experiences, but the experiences can be selected and simplified to help the child grasp the rules s/he needs to learn. Repeated demonstrations of actions with toys in play can clarify needed distinctions for a child, for example, between present and past tense, saying "The cow jumps" while moving the toy cow, then saying "The cow jumped" after completing the movement.

Planned language play is also invaluable because the approach sets up *fresh situations* that are free from the ingrained negative expectations and unproductive styles of interacting that have come to plague everyday relations. The core strategy of presenting language through interaction play with toys, as well as in the course of the basic care routines of dressing, eating, washing, and in looking at picture books, provides no expectations for how well or poorly the child is performing. Thus the time-worn negative expectations and responses do not come into play. If a child fails to choose an object asked for or to carry out an action requested (e.g., make a toy dog run), the caregiver has only to label the same and similar objects and actions at other times and in other places. The aim is to give a rich variety of examples of words and sentences, a few at a time, over a series of many sessions. From these examples, children will gradually learn to talk comfortably and proficiently (Note that children do not all necessarily progress steadily or step by step; often they make periodic leaps after days of apparently no improvement at all.) In any case, steady or not, there are few children in whom new levels of competence will not become evident after a few weeks. Good relations and encouragement are inherent to this strategy. In fact, ignoring wrong responses is also part of the process, as it is in the strategy of behavioral remediation. The *difference between the two strategies is that in cognitive strategies new material on language is brought in for the child to learn from*, and the material is broken down in simplified examples to make it easy for the child to grasp the rules. A caregiver also does not wait for positive expressions of language to reward the child. *All* of the child's manipulations in play, physical or linguistic, are rewarded by the full attention of the adult, who also rewards by selectively labeling the key components of children's activity—the objects and actions they are using in the situation. Because there is also something to label in every initiative (response in behaviorist language) children make, the interactions provide endless experiences of language and social reinforcement—but loaded with new knowledge about language as well.

DIAGNOSING PROBLEMS OF LANGUAGE DEVELOPMENT

Just how far behind is the child and in what way? It obviously makes a difference whether it is a three-year-old or an 18-month-old who has never been known to say any words at all; or whether the child says words, but never sentences, or uses disorganized or incomplete sentences, or merely articulates poorly and speaks haltingly.

Hearing Loss

Does your child not only never say any words but also seems not to understand much of what you say? Or perhaps never responds at all to words? Deafness, especially partial deafness, is not always easy to spot in young children, because up to a certain point they can learn to compensate by responding to the visual cues people make when saying something. For example, the child learns that the caregiver looks at the refrigerator when asking if the child wants some juice.

As in the case of learned helplessness, parents and other caregivers also sometimes learn modes of communicating with a deaf child that can mask and delay recognition of a child's deafness. This is particularly true of selective hearing loss, where the deafness blurs comprehension of certain speech sounds, such as voiceless consonants (e.g., p, t, f, k) or narrow vowels (e.g., i, e), thus delaying or distorting healthy speech development. Yet the child still responds in intelligible ways that make caregivers believe he or she understands but simply can't or won't make proper efforts.

Selective and other partial hearing losses are common culprits, because total hearing loss is likely to be noticed by adults even in the early months of infancy: the infant is not startled by sharp sounds, never turns to locate a noise or make any response to rattles, voices or any other sounds. Because day care teachers work with groups of children, they are less likely to develop the compensatory communication devices parents may fall into. Partial hearing losses are thus frequently spotted in older infants on their first entry to day care. Day care teachers may pick up losses even pediatricians miss because the range of demands for communication in day care furnishes opportunities for comparative observation not available with clinical assessment of the child alone.

Informal Evaluations

Informal hearing tests with a bell or a tuning fork can usually establish whether there is total or substantial hearing loss and in which ear, but parents and teachers may find it difficult to determine subtle forms and degrees of partial deafness. Try ringing a small bell or tuning fork two or three feet behind the child's head, when the child is sitting in a chair with his or her back toward you and cannot see you. Ring it first a foot or so to the left of center, behind the child's ear, then the same distance to the right of center. If there is no response, ring it a foot or less behind the ear, again first from one angle, then the other. If the child does respond well from both sides at two or three feet, test again at increasing distances, as far as across the room. It is helpful to take the test on yourself with the aid of a friend or another teacher to get some idea of what to expect from normal hearing (assuming your hearing is normal).

It may be necessary to make a few little tests at odd moments without setting them up in a formal way. Approach the child quietly from behind at a time the child does not know you are in the room. It may also be

Box 38
Checking for Hearing Loss in Older
Infants and Preschoolers

Signs in the Everyday Environment
- Child often fails to turn head in response to loud or sharp sounds.
- Child often fails to turn head in response to unusual or unexpected sounds.
- Child misunderstands words containing certain sound combinations (e.g., unvoiced consonants, higher pitched vowels, such as "ee").
- Child consistently mispronounces certain sound combinations.
- Child has difficulty communicating verbally with peers, or playing with them, apparently because of misunderstandings. Children's high pitched voices and incorrect pronunciations make a good test of selective hearing difficulties.
- Family/day care staff relies excessively on gestures to communicate with child.

Making Informal Tests
- Use devices that make distinctive sharp sounds, such as a bell or tuning fork.
- Sound the device, first a foot or two behind the child's head, then at increasing distances across the room. Make the sound first slightly to the left, then to the right to test hearing acuity of each ear separately.
- If the child is too young, anxious, or rebellious to cooperate, make the tests at different times on different days when the child is concentrating in play and unaware of your presence.

Seek Professional Advice if in Doubt
- Be sure a thorough evaluation is made by a trained specialist, such as a speech pathologist or audiologist.

necessary to run tests on several different occasions, because young children, especially those with hearing difficulties, can be quick to sense an adult's presence and frequently resist the formality of test situations. Once they feel something special is going on behind them, they may repeatedly turn around rather than cooperate.

If you feel assured the child is responding to the sounds of the bell (and not other cues) at a good distance, try testing the child's responses to speech. Give the child some simple instructions, like "Touch your ear," making sure it is something that the child understands. Give different instructions, using different degrees of loudness, from vigorous calls to barely audible whispers, and at different distances. Have others whose normal voices vary considerably in pitch perform the same experiments. Children's voices are useful for testing the high-pitched ranges.

If you can, try experimenting with a variety of contrasting speech sounds as well. For example, ask the child to repeat such contrasting words as *bet* and *pet*, *rat* and *fat*, *bit* and *pit*, and *pet* and *pit*, *bit* and *bat*, *man* and *nan*. Unfortunately, such exercises are difficult to ask infants to perform because of their limited vocabulary. Asking them to imitate single sounds, such as *p* then *b* or *d* followed by *t*, may work better. Or place pairs of objects in front of the child and ask for each object in turn (e.g., *bell* then *ball*, *can* then *car*), making sure you don't give visual cues for the word by looking at the object asked for. Even these simple tasks may be too difficult for infants and many preschoolers with limited vocabulary, however, so make sure that they can comprehend the task you are presenting.

If doubts persist about hearing loss, consult a pediatrician and ask for a complete formal evaluation from a specialist. The evaluation must be more complete than the informal tests just described. They should be administered by a trained audiologist or speech pathologist who can evaluate hearing across a range of frequencies, without confusing hearing loss with language delay. The poor language skills of delayed children often make it difficult in informal evaluations to distinguish between hearing loss and poor language comprehension.

Should serious loss of hearing be confirmed, be sure to ask the specialist to discuss all the options and resources available for treatment, including teaching the child sign language, perhaps in combination with learning to talk through special instruction.

A DEVELOPMENTAL PROFILE OF LANGUAGE DELAY

Once hearing loss is ruled out (or compensated for by hearing aids), the language difficulties themselves can be dealt with. At this point, diagnosing problems with language development for many children is essentially a matter of observing what level or stage of development the child has reached, as reflected in the child's common forms of speech errors. A profile of common errors at successive stages of development is outlined in Box 39, along with guides on what to do at each stage to correct the difficulties.

It will be noted that there are basically four main levels of delay (or stages at which delay occurs), in keeping with the major levels with which language is organized and whose differences in complexity determine the order in which they are acquired. Within these levels, certain types of error patterns, both those of omission and of incorrect use, are found. Language delayed children vary considerably in the types of difficulties they develop. The errors found at Level I, Sounds, are the omission of certain sounds or substitution of certain sounds for the correct ones. At the other extreme, Level IV, Themes, difficulties with language appear in the processes of accuracy and organization of passages of material. It is thus not enough to observe that a child is delayed or has difficulties with language communication. It is obviously essential to know something about what the difficulties are, and in what specific areas within the different levels the child's difficulties lie.

Language Learning is Cumulative and Interconnected

Yet language learning is also cumulative. However delayed they may be, children will make some kind of progress at all levels (unless the delay is recognized at an earlier stage), and the progress and error patterns they make at successive levels will build on whatever they have learned at the earlier levels. That is, statements children make are built up of sounds into words of different parts of speech which in turn are organized into phrases and sentences, and these are further organized into passages of discourse. This means that, assessing children's difficulties requires a look at their total communication pattern, checking them out for the different errors they may make at the different levels of analysis. Do they mispronounce certain words? Is their vocabulary limited? Do they mix up certain prepositions (e.g., *on* for *over*) or conjunctions (use *and* when they mean *or*)? Perhaps they constantly confuse antecedents, leaving the listener confused regarding what or who is performing an action and to what and to whom. Or phrases may frequently be mixed up, making the general stream of their efforts to tell about a series of happenings quite disorganized.

Box 39
Correcting Speech Problems at Different Stages of Delay

Stages & Ages of Delay	Some Common Error Patterns	Things to Do
I. Sounds After 14 Months	*Omissions:* Final consonants: Cluster reductions: (dog = do') (step = 'tep) *Substitutions:* Voicing-devoicing (pill=bill=pill) Stop-fricative (bag = zag) Front for back consonants (get=det) Glides for liquids (light=yight) *Assimilation* (doggy = goggy = doddy)	Play with words that use problem sounds Read/recite nursery rhymes/poetry Articulate clearly Use object word play, books, and routines, focusing on sounds in different contexts to aid generalizing

II. Words
 	
After 18
Months
	Simple Parts of Speech:
	Nouns: Verbs:
	    Limited Vocabulary
	        Wrong Use:
	Singular-Plurals Irregular-regular
	Over-under Tenses, persons
	generalizing Auxiliaries
		Labeling play: use
		nouns and verbs
		according to errors
		Focus on vocabulary
		building or giving
		models of correct
		usage as needed

	Complex Parts of Speech:
	Adjectives-Adverbs-Prepositions
	Articles-Conjunctions-Pronouns
	  Limited Vocabulary
	  Wrong Use:
	    Omissions
	    Substitutions within and
	    across categories
		Labeling play: focus on
		problem parts of speech
		Use clear, simple
		sentences that point up
		correct forms in varied
		ways and contexts to
		aid generalizing

As a result of this cumulative interdependency between levels in the hierarchy among sounds, words, sentences, and themes, the errors children make at one level are likely to affect how well they use the rules at the other levels; they are most often influences working from the lower to the higher levels. Thus children who tell things (themes) in a disorganized fashion do so at least in part because of errors they make in the lower level building blocks: They organize their sentences (syntax) poorly, which in turn is in part because of problems in choosing the correct parts of speech

---

Box 39 (cont.)

III. Phrases/ Sentences
 	
After 30 Months
	All Parts of Speech:
	Past the single words stage these errors often.involve both
	  (1) using the wrong term and
	  (2) confused syntactical relations
		Phrase-sentence play activities
		As for Stage II errors

	Errors of Syntax: Incomplete or confused relations and disorganization: Subject-predicate-object relations Antecedent relations Phrase-clause forms and relations Active-passive voice	Phrase-sentence play activities Focus attention on relational and organizational problems; show correct & varied forms with substitutions
IV. Themes After 4 years	Statements confused because of wrong parts of speech or syntax Incomplete or undeveloped material Unorganized or poorly connected statements Inaccurate or meaningless statements	Word-phrase-sentence play as for above Extended conversation & discussion Narrative activities (books, happenings, etc.

NB—Many language development problems are rooted in semantics (meaning): poor language experiences frequently mean the child's concepts about the world and thinking skills are also poorly developed. Remedial effort thus often requires enriching experiences and above all anchoring the language stimulation play in concrete activities that make meaning clear.

(word selection).

Using sounds correctly may, however, be relatively independent: The child who pronounces badly may otherwise be able to use grammar well and narrate in an orderly manner; and conversely, clear pronunciation is no guarantee of grammar and thematic organization. Children may also be relatively competent in using the different parts of speech, yet find it difficult to organize their ideas in sentences, which then influences how well they can narrate. Various other combinations are possible.

CORRECTING ERRORS AT DIFFERENT STAGES

Whatever the levels or errors of language difficulty, a fresh start that concentrates on illustrating the rules the child has difficulty with will usually make a difference. Specific guidelines for matching what to do with the child's needs are listed in Box 39. One way to go about the task is first to gather a number of samples of the child's speech, perhaps with the aid of a tape recorder, then noting down the main types of problems. It may be necessary to replay a tape several times to identify some of the more subtle forms of errors, especially if you are uncertain yourself about some of the correct forms. It is probably unnecessary to get all of the types listed clearly the first time, since one usually cannot attend to everything at once.

Correcting Errors at Stage I: Pronunciation

Assuming one main difficulty is with mispronunciation, reading and reciting verse and rhyme are excellent devices for improving articulation, as Box 39 indicates. Articulating more clearly oneself and playing with key words during the course of care routines and in other activities will also generally sharpen the child's attention to correct sound patterns. If the problem is with substituting *d* for *g*, for example, find verses that bring in alliteration, "Diddle, diddle Dumpling...", alternating this with "Higglety, Pigglety," and "dig down, down deep" alternating with "going, going, gone." Or use rhymes like *katydid, hid,* and *bid,* alternating with ones like *big, fig,* and *dig.* These alternations help to draw attention to the contrasting forms. Ones that require alternating *d*'s and *g*'s, such as "See the big girl dig the deep ditch with her green dog" are particularly useful and lots of fun. Start with short two- or three-word combinations like *big ditch* and *great dog,* to simplify the task and gradually expand it to ensure continued success and build confidence.

Repeating verses the infant enjoys will usually lead the child to try repeating them him or herself, often with gradually improving pronunciation. *It is important not to be too teachy or to seem to be concerned with correcting errors, which makes the child feel scolded or a failure.* Talking simply and reciting with enjoyment, good pronunciation, and lots of variety yields the best results. Above all, avoid pressing the child to perform. It will only increase resistance. And if children fail to perform correctly, it's seldom because they don't want to; it's usually because they don't know or can't easily apply the rule in question because an incorrect form has become ingrained or habitual. Time and practice with numerous examples that point to the difference between correct and incorrect forms will usually solve the problem in the long run. But keep in mind that if pronunciation is not the chief problem, it may be best to leave it aside and deal with the problems of other levels. If a child does not gradually improve in some way in a month or so, however, it may be wise to consult a speech therapist.

Correcting Errors at Stages II and III: Problems with Words and Sentences

Correcting errors in parts of speech and making sentences through play are in some ways easier and in some ways more difficult than correcting errors of pronunciation. It is easier because few of the errors are quite as automatic and unconscious as errors in pronunciation. But it is also more difficult because many of the problems involve rules that are closely tied to poor understanding of the relations and events that children try to describe in speech.

Errors often originate in semantics or meaning, as a result of the child's limited experience in concept development. For example, a child's failure to distinguish clearly between present, past, and future events is likely to cause difficulties in using verb tenses. Confusion about antecedents may be linked to an inability to conceptualize the different parts several persons and things play in a situation that the child tries to describe.

Using Language Play

It is for this reason that it is essential during language play to accompany the correct verbal forms with simple demonstrations of the activities and events represented. Interaction play with various replicas (animals, people, vehicles) and other objects is particularly valuable to demonstrate the specific rules about language. It is often easier to learn the rules through guided play than it is to learn them in the course of everyday activities. Ordinary events move from one thing to another so quickly that it is difficult to illustrate a rule before the next event arrives. In contrast, during play a caregiver can choose, demonstrate, organize, and label key elements of an activity, again and again, in many different ways and at a suitable pace.

Whatever a child's difficulties, take them on one at a time and give the child a wide variety of casual and pleasant experiences with examples that illustrate the rules that the child is having difficulty with. If the child is poorly developed in a large number of language rules, the problem is of course much broader in scope, and the efforts required necessarily greater. Still, as along as the activities are presented in a friendly, interactive form of play, and the rules are clearly illustrated one at a time, progress can generally be counted on. One can also take heart from the fact that it is not always essential to cover all the rules the child has problems with. Extended play with a few of the rules often leads children to become more aware of the existence of rules, which they then begin to learn on their own through observing and trying out the rules in their everyday interactions with others. This is the process of *learning to learn* described earlier, which so greatly facilitates children's cognitive development, once the child is given a solid foundation.

One of the great things about learning language is that it is available for learning every day, almost everywhere. The child only has to reach a certain level of competence and to understand generally what the task is, namely, that speech is organized according to rules that enable one to say in order to be understood clearly. Playing with the rules of language in precise and friendly ways gives children just this kind of awareness, which teaches them some of the rules; that in turn motivates them and gives them the tools to learn on their own. They will still benefit greatly from continuing guidance, but as they attain higher levels of mastery, caregivers will find the child more and more a collaborator and fellow initiator in the process of language (and other) learning.

Correcting Errors at Stage IV: Development Problems with Theme Learning

Problems at level IV, the level of narrating about things in connected themes, might seem the most difficult to solve. Yet in some ways they are the easiest because books and stories, which furnish excellent experiences in learning the complex rules of theme development, have such a strong appeal for children. Among these rules are the organization and development of a story line, in which events follow one another in time and the happenings of successive events relate to one another through the continuing actions and encounters of the actors. It is these sometimes very intricate story line qualities (especially those with several actors and various subplots) that draw children into the activity of hearing a story read or told to them. Somehow all of us delight in this most basic aspect of life, the unfolding of experience. When it is dramatized through the selective presentation of events to shed light on how people's choices and the nature of things lead to certain consequences, we identify the story events with our own life circumstances.

First Steps

Children, even little ones, do the same. The only proviso is that the story characters, events, and their connections be sufficiently close to their own experiences for them to follow the story line. For children who lack experience in language and books, for whatever reasons, as in the case of two- or three-year-olds who say no more than a few words and have rarely seen a book, the potential appeal for story themes still exists. It is only necessary to begin slowly, at the beginning, about where one would begin with a year old infant. Looking at books that picture no more than one or two objects on a page is a good place to start. Looking at books, gradually beginning to read the text, along with the labeling during play and care routines, will soon expand children's vocabulary and their ability to form sentences. Two- and three-year-olds, even language delayed ones, have had some kinds of experience in observing and manipulating the things in space around them, however, more than most one-year-olds. Thus they can frequently move quickly from words to sentences and from pictures of single objects to pictures of scenes and series of scenes depicting connected events more rapidly than a one-year-old might, provided a good relationship is established, provided the adult is sufficiently interactive and dramatic, and provided the child has not already become too activity oriented. Even if the child has, patience and persistence, varying one's techniques and diversifying and simplifying will often prevail. Many extreme cases of hyperactivity and other behavioral problems, of course, are likely to require professional assistance. But don't underestimate the potential of persistence in interactive play for improving the competence and self-esteem of many children in ways that will diminish their behavioral problems, which often arise from a sense of incompetence in the first place.

Remember, as interesting as stories may be, high activity children with little language experience have had little chance to imagine or even understand happenings in language forms. What we usually think of as "general cognitive development" or intelligence is heavily founded on the understanding that comes through competence in language, the ability to describe and conceptualize the world around us verbally. It is for this reason that we usually must help delayed children to develop skills at several levels simultaneously, with words, phrases and themes, and perhaps pronunciation, to help them catch up.

Expanding Theme Development

Once the child's interest in some story—any story— is held for even a brief period, the process of expanding theme understanding is only a matter of repeating the story experience. Gradually introduce stories with longer and more complicated plots—always making sure that the child's interest follows along. As with any normally stimulated infant, the delayed child will probably sooner or later begin to spontaneously comment on scenes, ask questions, and state what happens next. But like the normal child, the delayed child's participation in telling the story, which is the core of theme development skills, will be markedly accelerated if the adult pauses between events and encourages participation. Reading the same interesting tale over and over again and engaging the child in a dialogue will help. Also, remember not to pressure the child with repeated requests to perform. There is no substitute for a warm and easy relationship in which both adult and child feel they are jointly experiencing and talking about the events together, once the child comes to know a story well.

Telling About Things and Sociodramatic Play

Theme development also comes out of narrating about daily happenings and personal experiences, as discussed at length in the description of Stage IV activities in Chapter 9. It is wise, however, not to ask a child whose strengths have not been in language to now suddenly start telling about this and that, however dramatic the experience and apparently keen the child's interest. Given sufficient attention to language and story reading, even on this delayed basis, most children will sooner or later want to report events on their own, beginning with halting accounts of no more than a few disjointed sentences.

Making interesting opportunities available, taking time after interesting experiences to sit down with children and play with them, will accelerate the process. Before beginning the play or story reading, a brief pause and a comment about a recent happening may elicit some comment by the child, which if done from day to day will grow into more meaningful accounts. Soon both the caregiver and the child will be sharing in talking about what happened.

Sociodramatic play and trips and outings with playmates will also stimulate a child's interest in talking about things. At some point, once children have become confirmed story book listeners and regularly talk about the little things of daily life, they can be encouraged to make longer narratives and engage actively in storytelling to audiences of different sizes. Competence in language and theme development are now reasonably well assured.

Figure 11-1. *Keeping Records in Day Care: Adding a New Word to a Child's Record*

Chapter 11

Following the Infant's Progress: What Do You Measure?

Measuring how well children are learning language can be a complicated process, because there are so many rules to learn during the four different stages of development. What children can understand (comprehension) is also different from what they can say (production). Generally speaking, people understand more than they can say and children's understanding develops ahead of their ability to talk for a variety of reasons. The most important reason is because it is logically more difficult to express a thought through language than it is to understand what someone else has formulated in words. The former requires us to use language rules to compose an idea in words, while the latter is limited to the task of decoding the meaning of the language statements others have formulated.

Do You Test Infants or Observe What They Can Do?

But how do you make a comprehensive assessment of all these different aspects of language that constantly evolve over the course of early childhood? And how will a parent or teacher know that a certain kind of performance is adequate or slow, rich or impoverished compared to the development of other children in the culture? Perhaps a standardized mental test assessment is necessary, one that gives a separate measure of the child's competence in language. There are a number of mental scales that give a measure of language separate from the measurement of IQ or other abilities. Actually, the kind of informal records parents and day care staff can easily keep from day-to-day observations not only give a reasonably accurate and complete account of a child's development, but they provide the information in just the form needed, to *monitor* how and what the child is learning from day-to-day as language develops.

Advantages of Daily Observation over Formal Tests

While standardized language scales may give a more objective picture of development in terms of norms, they have several disadvantages. Many of them require a professional psychologist or other tester to administer and this can be expensive. And the results from one testing cannot match the kind of detailed process information that parents and teachers can get from observing a child's development daily over long periods. Moreover, the normative information covered in Box 2, Chapter 2, probably yields as much information as teachers and parents need to compare a child's development with norms. The ages for the early stages of learning sounds, words, and phrases are reasonably accurate within a range of two or three months or so, which is quite adequate, given that children generally progress unevenly at different points along the way. And children vary even more in the complex activities of talking in sentences, relating experiences and using the basic rules of grammar. After all, caregivers are most concerned with how a child is doing all along the way, not finding out just once, even if the assessment is precise and comprehensive. (The value of certain professionally designed language tests and scales that are relatively easy for nonprofessionals to understand and administer will be described briefly further on.)

How Well Does Performance on a Formal Test Measure the Child's Every Day Competence?

There is another distinction about language (or any other ability) in which direct observation in the home or day care may provide an advantage. What people are potentially *competent* to do is not always revealed in their *performance* at the moment they are assessed, and people, especially children, often perform differently from one situation to the next. Children usually perform best in familiar settings, like those of the home or day care, where they know what to expect and feel comfortable expressing themselves.

By their nature, mental tests are a formal experience in a strange setting with a strange person, even when conducted in an informal and relaxed manner. Procedures are by definition standardized, requiring a certain order and mode of eliciting selected information. The tasks the

Box 40
Measuring Language Development:
Formal Tests or Informal Observations?

Formal Tests

are Relatively Objective—

They give a relatively accurate picture of selected language skills at the child's current age, compared to other children in the culture through being:

Standardized on large samples of a general population with:

a. Sample skills that are supposed to indicate overall development,

b. In a standard, unfamiliar situation to obtain an average good performance,

c. With usually one, or at most several, testings to obtain samples at certain points in development to get a general idea of how the child's development is progressing

d. Frequently using a trained professional, who employs skill to ensure a standardized procedure and compensates for his/her strangeness to the child

Informal Observations

are Relatively Personalized and Comprehensive—

They furnish a series of detailed pictures of each child's development in many different language skills at many points in development by:

Observing children directly:

a. Performing a wide variety of the skills they acquire,

b. In common situations that embrace the total range of their competencies,

c. Repeatedly, daily, as long as desired throughout development to yield cumulative records, and provide constant feedback for caregivers to improve their methods of language stimulation

d. Using as observers parents, day care teachers, or other familiar figures with whom the child will perform "naturally" with minimal anxiety

Note:- Certain types of relatively standardized measures of language development can be used by nonprofessionals and administered repeatedly at monthly intervals because they are relatively simple to administer and inexpensive, though they do not have the scope and flexibility of direct observation. (See text for discussion of REEL and other similar Scales.)

child is asked to perform represent a standardized sample of the kinds of tasks the average child in the population has been found able to perform *in this kind of formal test situation.* This approach imposes a certain framework that does not allow children to present the things they know in the way they know them. They may have a vocabulary not well represented on a standardized test; their pronunciation may be difficult for an unfamiliar tester to understand; and above all their tensions in the strange situation may hamper their ability to perform. Children also vary from day to day and by time of day, fatigue, slight illness, and mood.

For all these reasons, observing how children perform at home or in day care often provides measures of their skills closer to their actual competence. Because children perform differently from day to day even at home, repeated observations make it possible to catch the child's best performance, thus giving the best measure of the child's competence for that period of development. Repeated observations, moreover, can also cover the range of situations and relations children experience in their total ecology to yield the full depth and variety of their performance capabilities. Continual observations furnish an important basis for improving the quality of the child's language stimulation, which will be discussed later in the chapter.

All in all, behavioral observations in the context of the familiar milieu in which the child lives will give a much broader, more rounded, detailed and evolving picture of the child's progress than one can ever get from a one-time test. The latter may be better for comparing the development of groups of children, for survey and some research purposes, but not for families and day care practitioners, or even for in depth research.

LEARNING RULES

Language Learning is Cumulative, But on a Zig-Zag Course

Language does not develop in a straight line. The child does not learn bits of information such as sounds and words one step at a time. Progress is irregular. The very fact of stages, with different categories of language from sound to theme skills to be mastered, tells us that language learning is not a simple process of adding on more and more units of the same type. Language is constructed of a vast network of rules, from the rules for combining sounds to the rules of grammar, each of which children appear at times to make sudden leaps to learn.

The Gradualness of Learning

Actually, new rules are not suddenly mastered in single big leaps. These apparent leaps are preceded by periods of gradually becoming familiar with various examples of a rule without clearly understanding the rule. For example, in learning their first words, children appear first to identify several objects by their individual names, usually highly valued people or things like mama and dada, or the pet cat, Sadie (an actual case) that are important to them in their daily life. This development often takes many weeks.

Soon they label two or three other important toys or objects they play with every day that are repeatedly labeled for them, such as their special ball someone uses in play with them or the cuddly stuffed dog they cherish. The word cookie is a frequent early candidate but even it is not understood as the name of all kinds of cookies in all circumstances. It is more likely to be understood as the sound patterns associated with the sweet things a parent gives to the child in the kitchen. Thus other balls, dogs, and cookies that appear in different sizes, shapes, colors, and circumstances will not immediately be linked with the relevant sound patterns. It takes time and repeated experiences before the child begins to generalize.

Making a Synthesis: Coming to Understand a Rule

Gradually, children begin to see connections between the examples and they suddenly seem to make a big leap in understanding. They make a synthesis that enables them to grasp the general rule. They do this because, at some point, after extended experience with many different examples, they seem to suddenly put it all together. That is, they gradually become aware of the special characteristics that define each *type* of object with which they have associated labels for a few examples. Thus they eventually become aware that all balls are round and roll, that dogs have four legs, big ears, big mouths, and a tail, and that cookies are all flat, crumbly and sweet—and that the other characteristics of these objects, their size, shape, color and the circumstances in which they are seen (at home or somewhere else) don't count. To paraphrase Gertrude Stein: A cookie is a cookie is a cookie...

Once children have understood the general rule about word labels in terms of two or three words, they begin to apply them to new examples of the objects they encounter. Still the process is gradual. At first they may see only other small balls as being a ball like their special ball, or only another toy dog that looks like their own stuffed dog as a dog. Big balls and real dogs may take longer for them to see the resemblance, because they have other characteristics, that make them so different. Experience with new examples is a process of consolidating and extending their understanding of the rule that defines the characteristics of each object that has a certain name. Obviously, examples that are widely different in their characteristics from common examples take longer to learn. What children are consolidating is their understanding of the *general idea or rule about words, all words, standing for types of things.*

Learning Follows a Cyclical, But Accelerating Course

One can see that there are alternating phases of incremental and transformational (rule) learning for different phases of comprehension. In understanding words, first, children become acquainted with the bits and pieces of a very few special objects that are labeled for them. A big leap comes next, when children make a mental synthesis of how labels are applied to types of objects according to selected characteristics. This mental synthesis then enables children to move again in increasingly rapid steps, but on new levels and in new ways. They can now apply knowledge of this general rule to recognize the labels of endless numbers of word-object associations, which is done in incremental steps in understanding word units with increasing rapidity. At an early stage of understanding, however, infants begin to try to imitate, and then say words on their own. In both cases this begins slowly, then gradually accelerates. And by the time they have mastered about 20 words, they have acquired enough examples of how words can be combined into sentences to begin forming sentences of gradually increasing length.

Learning the other concepts of language at the different stages follows the same cyclical, accelerating course. In learning sounds, one of the bases for learning words, infants learn to recognize and synthesize sounds into strings to make words. They progress from making single sounds to combining sounds in repetitive babbling, first repeating the same two-unit syllables, then different syllables, and finally making sets of sounds they connect with meaning to make words.

Children come similarly to understand the different parts of speech, first static objects (nouns), like ball and dog, then concrete actions (verbs) like walk and kiss, and then the other more complex ones like adjectives and pronouns. Learning these other rules follows the same irregular accelerating course: First, children slowly become familiar with easy examples, until they arrive at a more or less general understanding. Then they apply each of the rules as they are mastered to more and more examples with increasing rapidly. Almost any different language rule learning process can be displayed in graphs like those shown in Box 41.

Children Progress at Different Rates, Though All Follow the Same Accelerating Zig-Zag Course

How rapidly children learn new examples for rules, that is new words (or sounds or sentences), will depend greatly on the quality of the guidance in learning language they get from their caregivers. Giving children lots of clear examples, labeling them carefully and often in play and other routines, and showing children the resemblances between objects sharing the same label will advance the process of understanding the rule. Children who are left to their own devices have to make inferences on their own. It may take them many months to gradually build up their first real vocabulary of 20 or 30 words. Children enjoying enriched language environments, on the other hand, who may take a couple of months to say mama, dada, ball, dog, and cookie, will learn several more words inside a couple of weeks, 20 words in another month and soon so many words that it is virtually impossible to keep track of their vocabulary learning. These rates of learning can be shown in what are called cumulative learning curves as seen in Box 41, which shows several such curves for a well-stimulated infant in one of our research projects.

These include his curves for understanding and imitating words, as well as for saying them, and also for sentences of increasing length, all of which follow much the same zig-zag accelerating course of development.

The discussion on delayed language development in the previous chapter underscores how children do not progress at the same rates. Box 42 compares the average rates for saying words for infants exposed to different quality language environments. But notice, regardless of the differences between rates, that all children have a relatively slow beginning, gradual increase, then an accelerating rate of word acquisition in the later stages. The richer the language environment, the more rapid the acceleration, as the figure in Box 42 makes clear, but fast or slow, according to experience, learning to say words is not a straight line, nor a steady rate of development. The first words said come slowly, through

Box 41
Cumulative Learning Curves for Word and Phrase Development in an Infant from a Highly Stimulating Language Environment

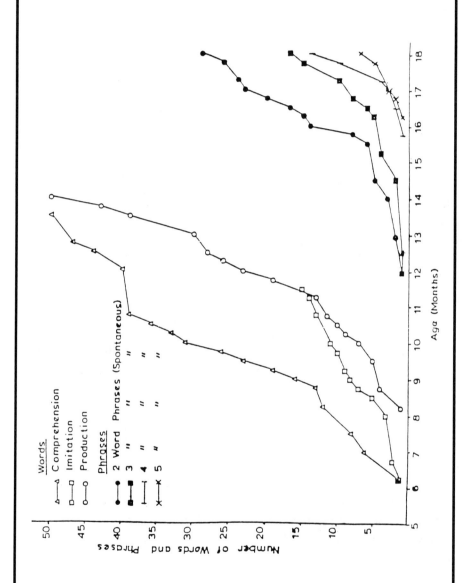

(Showing Accelerating Rates and Zig-Zag Course Development)
Adapted from Figure 4, Fowler & Swenson (1979)

this gradual process of familiarizing, which is represented by the long shallow slope. The sharp change in direction upward in the curves reflects the child grasping the general rule about word labeling. The final steep slope upward records how the child can now apply this knowledge to other labels of other things with increasing rapidity.

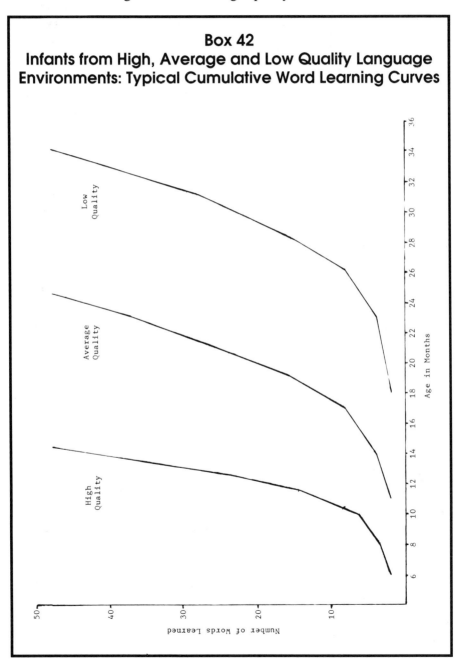

Box 42
Infants from High, Average and Low Quality Language Environments: Typical Cumulative Word Learning Curves

WAYS OF MEASURING CHILDREN'S PROGRESS

The bulk of the methods for measuring children's progress in learning language to be described will consist of measures that describe the child's language behavior. In other words, they are records of observations detailing what the child actually achieves. These methods are all relatively easy to carry out, though they require a certain amount of consistent attention. The records obtained can be used to give as simple or as complex an assessment of language development as one might want, depending upon the different resources of parents or day care staff.

Professionally Designed Measures

Although formal measures are not always available to nonprofessionals, many are easy to use. Among the simplest for teachers and parents to use is the **REEL Scale** (Bzoch and League, 1971), which assesses children's development of understanding and speech separately. Caregivers simply check off the behaviors that describe a child's patterns, organized in common monthly steps of development, thus directly yielding a developmental age, indicating whether a child is advanced, behind or average in terms of norms.

Other measures include: The **MacArthur** (Fenson et al., 1993) is organized into check-off lists to inventory communication skills, assessing words and gestures (8 to 16 months) and words and sentences (16 to 30 months). It includes diverse categories of vocabulary, and elements of syntax, grammar and social play. The **Brigance** (1978) provides a shorter skill inventory of age-graded pre-speech and speech and language items (birth to age 7), along with an assessment of motor, self-help, knowledge and academic skills. The **Miller and Paul** (1994) provides an unusual in-depth clinical inventory of children's understanding of language from 8 months to 10 years. Finally, the **Peabody** (Dunn, 1965), is more of an IQ test than a developmental scale. It measures comprehension vocabulary through pictures, but only starts at 2 1/2 years, then extends to age 18. It is also standardized on a broader sample. Because the scales describe each of the steps quite clearly, they shed insight on what the child needs to know next. These and other professional scales can be located through educational libraries or texts on child development and language development.

Audio and Videotaping

Audio tape recorders are now widely found in many homes and other settings and video cameras are increasingly common, as the price of the new technology gradually declines. The widespread use of videocassette players in the home makes consideration of a video camera for any family wishing to have a fascinating audiovisual record of their child's development a real possibility. Both audio and video techniques will furnish extensive samples of language competence at any give point in time, but each has certain advantages and disadvantages.

Audio recording is much simpler and less expensive to use than video recording, but it lacks the visual picture needed to assess the child's competence in understanding language (*language comprehension*). Visual cues are also useful for the viewer to determine the full meaning of what the child is saying (*language production*). For example, to find out whether a child understands the meaning of a word, such as "wastebasket", one has to *see* whether the child points to or otherwise indicates a wastebasket visually when someone says the word, as in asking the child to point to it. And, when talking while playing with blocks, for example, because one can't see the actions one can't always tell whether the child is using words accurately (e.g., the child says "Let's put the square block behind the long one here.").

Whichever technique is employed, tape recording is a method of collecting a representative sample of the child's language at different points in development. Because taping, transcribing, and evaluating the records are time consuming and because there is usually little change from day to day, taping more than once every week or two is not necessary. Taping may not work well at all during the early stages of sound and word learning, as infants will seldom reproduce on demand the new rules they are still consolidating. Capturing the new expressions, which appear only at odd moments throughout the day, requires the use of the kind of running records to be described shortly.

The richest language samples usually begin to emerge in Stage III, as children begin to talk in increasingly longer and more varied phrases and use more and different grammatical rules. Still, change usually comes slowly and the most obvious change, their rapidly expanding vocabulary, requires taping in the different situations they are known to be familiar with to collect the increasing variety in their vocabulary content. Even then, keeping a running list of new words is about the only way of approaching the enormous multiplication of new words, once the child passes the early stages of word learning.

Importance of Planning and Preparation

In the end, everything really depends on how much parents or teachers want to know, and how much time they are willing to devote to these efforts. It must be repeated, however, that each hour of taped material will usually take several hours to collate and analyze.

Collecting rich language samples from little children requires preparation. Spontaneous taping is seldom feasible because it usually interrupts the activity. A safer method is to bring together a selected set of play materials of the type listed in Box 7, Chapter 5, to engage the child in interactive play with someone capable of leading the play in a variety of directions. As children begin to talk they will spontaneously talk about the things they are playing with. One simply follows the same principles of interaction used in the everyday play sessions for stimulating language development. Using a variety of different toys (animal figures, vehicles, common objects) and taping in different activities (toy play, looking at books, care routines) and settings (kitchen, bedroom, yard, day care) will widen the range of vocabulary and ideas sampled. The play setting should be comparatively informal and free from disturbing distractions and interruptions.

A Good Measure of Later Language Development: Sentence Length or Mean Length of Utterance (MLU)

The length of each taping session varies according to the detail and scope of material desired. From 10 to 30 minutes is typical, depending on how fluently the child talks during a session. One of the commonest measures of language development, the child's **mean length of utterance (MLU)**, or the average length of statements used, is based on counting the average number of words in each sentence (whether or not complete) over a total of 100 responses (Brown, 1973). (Technically, one counts the number of morphemes, which counts variations for word inflections like plurals and tenses as additional units.) The 100 responses are usually counted after the child gets going, say after 10 responses or two to three minutes or so, and should not include any recitations (e.g., memorized nursery rhymes). While some parents or teachers may want to utilize all criteria from the original definition, for most it is probably enough simply to count the number of words or word approximations, excluding repetitions and stuttering.

What to expect in terms of norms is shown in Box 43, which are samples of well-stimulated children from educated families runs from around 1.2 at 18 months to 5.3 by age 6. Counting by words instead of morphemes, incidentally, will produce shorter MLU's than those shown in Box 43, which are calculated using morphemes.

Other Formal Measures:
Longest Sentence, Type/Token Ratio and Grammar

Highly stimulated children might be expected to produce an MLU of more than 1.0 as early as 12 to 16 months of age, accelerating past these norms thereafter. Less well-stimulated children would of course fall behind to varying degrees, in some cases producing MLUs of no more than 2.0 by age 3 or even 4.

There is hardly any limit to the variety of information about children's language these tapings can yield, at least once they begin to talk in sentences and assuming that they talk more or less freely during a play session. Many measures will be more complex and technical than most practitioners will want or need. Two additional useful and relatively

---

Box 43
Average Length of Children's Sentences
During the Early Years (Mean Length of utterances)

Children from Educated Families: Ages 18 to 60 Months

Age	18	21	24	27	30	33	36	39	42	45	48	51	54	57	60
MLU	1.2	1.4	1.9	2.4	2.7	2.7	3.7	4.2	3.7	4.2	4.3	4.5	4.7	5.2	5.3

Adapted from Miller and Chapman (1981). Note that children do not develop evenly in regular increases from age to age, as indicated especially by the exceptional level (4.2) shown for the 39 months age group. Your child is also likely to vary slightly from the mean levels shown at various ages, as a result of differences in background and experience.

simple ones are the child's longest utterance or sentences in a given taping session (or perhaps the 10 longest sentences) and the type/token ratio, which is the number of different words compared to the total number of words used in a session. The child's longest sentence gives a better estimate of a child's maximum potential, while the type/token ratio tells you how rich the child's vocabulary is.

Certain parents and day care teachers may be interested in using a few of the more complex measures, however, to gain detailed information on the development of the number and types of different parts of speech and other grammatical forms children use and the frequency and type of errors they make. The technique of **Developmental Sentence Analysis** is a professionally designed measure for analyzing in elaborate detail children's developmental progress in the complexity of their grammar (Lee, 1974). It is constructed in terms of two forms or levels, one for analyzing *Developmental Sentence Types (DST)*, which is appropriate for the early stages before the child makes complete sentences, and the other, *Developmental Sentence Scoring (DSS)*, which is to be used for analyzing the child's grammatical construction after reaching the stage of forming complete sentences a high proportion of the time. Still other professionally designed measures can be found by consulting some of the many

PHOTO BY SARAH PUTNAM

Figure 11-2. A Rich Variety of Toys/Will Help Build A High Type/Token Ratio

books on language development.

But such elaborate procedures many not be of interest to most caregivers, either in the home or day care. Adults with some knowledge of grammar can simply count what they think is the useful number and variety of adjectives, adverbs, prepositions, and other parts of speech children use, and of the use and correctness they make of plurals, tenses, auxiliaries, active-passive voice, and other grammatical forms.

Measures of Theme Development: Variety and Complexity

Audio and videotaping also furnish a good method for assessing theme development. Most caregivers are quite likely to be satisfied evaluating *variety*. This is done by simply estimating the number of themes children use by listening to a series of taping sessions and noting the number of different topics that come into the narrations or conversations. Much depends on the settings in which the taping is done, however. Unless tapings are deliberately planned in relation to experiences in different settings and activities, and the caregiver leads the theme activity in different directions, such as varying the topics of conversations following visits to different places (e.g., construction sites, zoo, train station), little variety is likely to enter into the narrations.

In many ways, measuring theme development is thus likely to be closely tied to the week-to-week activities of theme stimulation in which the child is involved. Perhaps the best solution is to periodically tape the storytelling or other activities in which the child is engaged. If children are taped from time to time in all of the different types of theme activities— telling about experiences, storytelling, sociodramatic play and the like— the variety of types of theme development are built into the taping. The variety of topics will of course depend on how varied the theme experiences. Usually, once a month or so is likely to be often enough, because theme skills do not develop as rapidly as vocabulary and sentence skills do. Taping is also a time-consuming activity. Once a month, assuming a variety of activities are sampled, is likely to easily fulfill the needs of most busy parents and practitioners.

But what about *complexity*? The easiest estimates are obtained by noting the length of children's narrations, and how they progress from month to month, which give some idea of how easily and fluently the child strings sentences together to make themes.

A more elaborate approach is to note how well children have ordered their material as they tell about some experience or topic. Transcribing or typing up the oral records will make it easier to make these analyses. Measuring complexity can, like evaluating grammatical development, become quite elaborate, extending even into the kind of quality assessments English teachers make in judging children's oral presentations or compositions. How elaborate and detailed are the stories or narrations? Are they repetitious, concise, and clearly presented? How pointed, well documented, and logically developed are the themes? How original and imaginative? Does the child introduce images and metaphor? Is the child stronger in talking about some themes than others?

Here we get into what areas of interest the child is developing. The important thing is not that children become skilled and fluent in everything talked about, but that they show strengths and persisting interest in some areas in ways that makes them want to actively contribute in shaping the future course of their development and life activity.

DAILY RECORDS OF INFANTS' LANGUAGE ACHIEVEMENTS

In our research, we have found that certain brief records of the child's day-to-day achievements in speech and understanding are about the easiest and most useful for parents and day care staff to maintain. On the one hand, they give caregivers a running account of a child's progress that furnishes constant information on how well things are going, and whether a change of method or course is in order. On the other hand, they can be compiled into graphs like those in Boxes 41 and 42 that give a cumulative, long-term picture of the child's development.

The record forms that we have devised take no more than a few minutes a day to maintain once the record forms are prepared and posted in some convenient work place, where the caregiver spends a good deal of her or his time (e.g., kitchen, children's play areas) with the child or children. They do however require a little effort and consistency for caregivers each day and for that reason not all families or day care staff will maintain them, useful as they may be. Some caregivers would find the occasional effort required to audiotape (or even videotape) a child's performance more rewarding, even though the latter may take more effort to set up a play situation, do the taping and analyze the results.

There are a number of different types of running records. The most common and useful are records of a child's progress in understanding and saying sounds, words and phrases/sentences. A convenient form used in our research for recording progress in the development in sound patterns is presented in Box 45.

Record of First Sounds (Stage I, Chapter 6)

The form is organized into a number of columns, with spaces at the top of the page to complete identifying information, especially useful at later periods when the exact circumstances are forgotten. The first column to the left is for listing all new sounds the child is heard to say for the first time. Some of these sounds will appear during the course of Stage I vocalization play with a caregiver, as infants imitate new sounds the caregiver brings into the interaction and spontaneously try out new ones on their own. Others will appear at odd moments when infants are playing

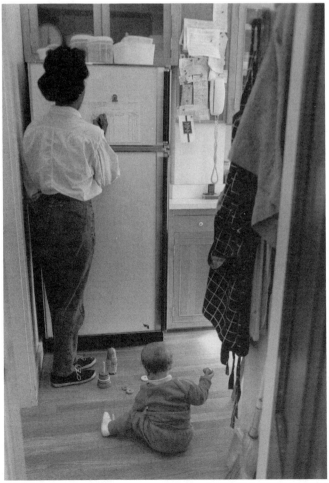

Figure 11-3.
The refrigerator is often a convenient place for keeping records in the home

PHOTO BY CATHY HOLAHAN

Box 44
What to Record

Basic Dimensions:

Sounds	*Words*	*Phrases/Sentences*
First 10 - 25 (Until words begin to emerge)	First 50: -understood -imitated -said alone (phrases begin at about 20 words said)	First 10 - 25: -understood -imitated (if any) -constructed alone (2 to 5 word units)

These are close to the maximum number of sounds, words and phrases that can be recorded easily. Beyond these limits, infants increase the rate at which they learn new terms so fast it is difficult to keep track of them all.

Any of the Many Other Language Rules:

Parts of Speech: First uses of nouns, verbs, prepositions, adverbs, conjunctions, articles, pronouns.

Variations in each of the different parts of speech may also be charted by the more technically minded, such as:
  Plural of nouns
  Verb tenses, case endings, use of auxiliaries, copula (verb "to be"), and irregular forms
  Comparisons of adjectives and adverbs
  Use of demonstratives, interrogatives, and other forms

Other developments in syntax may also be of interest to some caregivers, such as:
  Phrase expansions (the bus = the big bus = the big yellow bus)
  Causal expressions (because, since)
  Active and passive voice (Mary gave it to John = John got it from Mary)

Box 45

Early Vocalization Record (Pre-Word Development)

Infant's Name: _____

Birth Date: _____

Age of Starting: _____

Sex: _____

(1) Sound(s) or Syllables	(2) Date First Used	(3) Sounds Being Imitated-I/D* (if any)	(4) Comment: What was going on?	Date of Second Use	(5) Frequency of Use — How Often		
					1-2 times	3-5 times	Over 5 times
		*Immediate/ Delayed					

with sounds alone, lying down, perhaps playing with their toes or a mobile. Be sure to write down every new sound or combination of sounds the infant is heard to express, making the best written approximation of what you believe he or she vocalized. It is not necessary to use any formal phonetic code, just write down the combination of letters you believe best represents the sounds.

The date each sound or combination of sounds is first used is recorded in column 2 and what sounds the child may have imitated, and whether the imitation was immediate or delayed for a few minutes in column 3. Column 4 asks "What was going on?" It is for recording specifics, according to the kind of detail one wishes to keep, such things as whether (and to whom) the infant seemed to be communicating, what the setting and circumstances were, what the infant and the caregiver (if any) were doing, what the infant's mood was, and perhaps (at later stages) what the infant was trying to say (in words). The last column 5 is for indicating how often infants use a sound or sound combination, once they used it the first time, to give some idea of whether they have made it part of their repertoire.

Record of First Words (Stage II, Chapter 7)

Progress in word learning is recorded in much the same way, except that the child's progress in understanding words is also recorded. Word learning also opens wide possibilities for observing and recording details about the meaning(s) the child intends in using a word. Information about word progress is also kept in columnar form, with the same sort of identifying information, as shown in Box 46.

The first column to the left is for listing each new word the infant gives evidence of understanding, and column 2 for listing each new word spoken for the first time, with the date for first understanding or speaking recorded in column 3. If a new word appears to be an imitation, the word or words the child is imitating are recorded in column 4, along with a notation as to whether the imitation was immediate or delayed. Delays of more than a few minutes are probably words said independently. It is important to note down *every* new word the child appears to understand or say, even when the evidence or the word said is unclear. Later development or reviews of the records often help the caregiver identify just what the child was understanding or trying to say. Just record what you *believe* the infant understood or said in the best way you can (without worrying about phonetic coding). At least you will have a record that can

Box 46

Early Word Record (Single Word Development)
Words Understood and Words Said
Stage II

Infant's Name: _____ Sex: _____

Age of Starting: _____ Birth Date: _____

(1) Words Under-stood[a]	(2) Words Used (Spoken)	(3) Date First Under-stood/ Used	(4) Words Infant Imitated-I/D[b] (For Words Used)	(5) Comment: What was going on?	(6) Frequency of Understanding/Use			
					Date of Second Under-standing/ Use	How Often		
						1-2 times	3-5 times	Over 5 times
			[b] Immediate/ Delayed					

[a] Evidence child understood: Give an instruction like, "Feed the dolly," or "Put the cup on the table." Be sure the child is not getting hints from your actions or expression

be used later for evaluation.

Providing Evidence of Understanding

Evidence of whether an infant is really understanding or just responding to visual cues is not always easy to determine. A caregiver may feel that an infant understands some word, failing to realize that children will get a cue if they see an object when it is named, as when infants are handed their bottle or some toy (e.g., a rattle). If an infant's face lights up when someone says, well before bringing out the bottle, "Do you want your *bottle?*" one is still not sure whether it's the expectant look on the caregiver's face and the time of day that is giving the message, particularly for something as valued as the infant's bottle.

Sure evidence requires three things: (1) the infant must choose the object named by someone from among at least two objects; (2) the person saying the word must give no sign of which is the named object by looking at or pointing to the correct choice; and (3) the objects must not be placed so that the named object is placed in some preferred position the infant is likely to choose. Fulfilling these requirements is not so complicated as it may seem.

When parents or teachers get a hint that the infant understands one or two words, besides mama, dada, and the name of other family members or teachers, they may want to *set up a little play test.* Place 2 to 4 toys in front of the infant, including an example of the object whose name you believe the infant understands (e.g., ball), and ask the child to get or give you the *ball.* Do it several times, each time moving the objects around to different positions, but be sure to keep the activity informal and playlike. Frame different questions, such as, "Can you find the *ball?*" and "Where's the *ball?*" just as you would in ordinary word learning play activities, and don't pressure the child to perform. If the child gets it right each time, you can be fairly sure it is not just by chance. On the other hand, if the infant gets it wrong some of the time, it may simply be because the child doesn't feel like "playing this game," so drop it until another time.

Another method is to ask an infant to find a familiar toy across a crowded room, being sure not to look in the direction of the toy. Because of the distance—out of immediate sight—this is a more difficult task.

After showing signs of understanding several words, and about the time infants begin to say words, there will be little question about which ones they understand. They will have consolidated the idea of word learning and understanding, and will easily pick a named object from a set.

Recording the Circumstances

In the center of the form, column 5 is used for recording comments on "What was going on?" the circumstances surrounding the infant's apparent understanding or use of a new term. One of the important uses of these descriptions is the aid they give parents on whether a child really understands a certain word, as just described, and on what (if any) word the child is trying to say. The early pronunciation patterns of infants are often unclear and difficult to follow, even for parents, unless parents have

Figure 11-4. *"Can you get the giraffe?"*

Figure 11-5. *"That's it! You got the giraffe."*

PHOTOS BY SARAH PUTNAM

Administering a Play Test

made an effort themselves to articulate well in the word learning play. Writing down just what seems to have been happening, whom the infant was speaking to (if anyone), what he or she was playing with or what someone else just said sometimes clarifies the word the infant was trying to say.

The last column, column 6, is for recording just how often the child appears to understand or say new words. As with sounds, this record will give some idea of how well and how rapidly words are being incorporated into the infant's permanent repertoire.

Record of First Phrases and Sentences (Stage III, Chapter 8)

Keeping records of the infant's first phrases and sentences follows procedures very similar to keeping sound and word records, as seen in Box 47. The only difference is that units understood or spoken refer to phrases and sentences, rather than sounds or words. Otherwise, the same column sequence of units understood, spoken, the date, whether imitated, "What was going on?" and a record of how often the phrase/sentence appear to be understood or spoken is used.

Danger of Missing First Phrases and Sentences: The Child's Increasing Mobility and Use of Private Speech

It is easier to miss the first phrases and sentences children say, however, than it is to miss their first sounds and words. They spend more time in different settings—in play groups or day care away from home. Their growing mobility and cognitive skills also enable toddlers to play alone more and experiment with language on their own. Many children go through a phase of saying everything that comes to mind out loud. This is called a sort of private speech, first recognized by the Russian psychologist, Vygotsky (1962), in which children express ideas verbally by practicing aloud with the different language rules they are learning. Gradually this practice drops out as they master the code. Expressing thought through language becomes more or less automatic and silent in a shorthand form, except when talking aloud to communicate with others. Thinking aloud continues to some degree into adulthood, more in some persons than others, particularly when trying to work alone on a difficult problem.

Box 47
Early Phrase and Sentence Record (Two or Four or Five Word Combinations)
Phrases/Sentences Understood and Phrases/Sentences Said
Stage III

Infant's Name: _____   Sex: _____   Birth Date: _____

Age of Starting: _____

(1) Phrase/ Sent. Under- stood[a]	(2) Phrase/ Sent.s Used (Spoken)	(3) Date First Under- stood/ Used	(4) Phrases/Sent Imitated-I/D[b] (For Phrases/ Sent. said	(5) Comment: What was going on?	Date of Second Under- standing/ Use	(6) Frequency of Understanding/Use		
						How Often		
						1-2 times	3-5 times	Over 5 times
		[b] Immediate/ Delayed						

a Evidence child understood: Ask "Where is the _____?" or say "Give/bring/get me the _____."
   Be sure there is more than one thing to get and that the child is not getting hints from your actions or expression

Find Places to Observe Unobtrusively

Thus, collecting good records of sentence development requires alertness to the times and places toddlers may be playing with language by themselves. Is there a favorite spot your toddler goes to play for a few minutes every now and then, perhaps when he or she sees you are busy or preoccupied with something else? Chances are it is just down the hall or in a nearby room, as infants do not like to stray far from the scene of adult activity.

Even in day care, talking occurs more in some activities and areas of the playroom than others. It occurs most frequently in social play, but much depends on the loquaciousness of the child's habitual playmates, as well as the skill of the day care staff in shaping the quality and variety of the children's sociodramatic play.

Since toddlers are frequently not self-conscious about talking to themselves, they are often not disturbed by your observing them talking in play, unless your sudden presence intrudes or arouses their desire for adult attention or if a child is prone to seek adult attention constantly and has difficulty playing alone or with other children. In any case, listening to the chatter may sometimes give you examples of new experimental phrases you've never heard before. "Daddy go" may become "Shaggy go" (the family dog) and "Baby get up" may turn into "Dolly get up" or "Baby get down." It is even possible that missed chances to overhear private speech loses forever an infant's jump from using two word combinations to his/her first three-word construction, such as converting "Daddy come" to "Daddy come home."

Some children like to talk about things, lying in their crib as they are falling asleep at naptime or at night (Weir, 1962). Listening or placing a tape recorder at the bedroom door may yield a few surprises. Some children prefer always to play within sight of the adults, making it easier to keep an eye open for this stream of spontaneous language experimentation. Alertness to these possibilities is all that is required.

Imitations May Vary From What Someone Said. Any imitations the child makes may vary from the exact wording of the phrase or sentence someone else says, because the child does not quite understand. For example, she or he may get the tense wrong, want to express a slightly different meaning, or simply want to experiment and say it a little differently. Estimating just what phrases or sentences the child understands is also more complicated than determining words understood. A single word can be uttered alone, but phrases and sentences contain more than one word, making it sometimes difficult to know which ones the child does and does not know.

There is really no way around this short of setting up a complicated series of little tests, in which alternatives for each word are inserted each time, a process that may not interest many parents and practitioners. For example, one can ask the child to choose between "The *big* car" and "The *little* car," "mommy *walk*" and "mommy *run*," and even "Give it to *her*" and "Give it to *him*," making sure that no hints are given from your actions.

Record of Theme Development
(Stage IV, Chapter 9)

Because theme development progresses relatively slowly, daily records of theme progress serve little useful purpose. Measuring how children progress in the variety and complexity of their theme development was discussed above at the end of the section on audio- and videotaping.

Keeping Track of What You Say

Among the most useful records of language stimulation are those of when and where the baby is stimulated and a list of the actual words used in the language activities.

Frequency of Caregiver Talk. The easiest method is to keep a count of the number of language sessions the infant is offered each week. Listing all the different types of activities in which language is freely used, as shown in Box 48, gives a pretty good idea of how much clear language the child is being exposed to, and where the richest experiences are.

Tallying the Number of Sessions. All you need to do is to make a tally mark after finishing each session, placing marks opposite the appropriate activity area (listed in the left column). It helps to keep tally sheets handy where the care routines and other activities occur most frequently. Marks made on different sheets can be added up at the end of the week, without bothering to transfer anything but the totals to a single master sheet.

Keeping Time Records. If you want to keep more detailed information, you can note the number of minutes for each session. The total number of

Box 48

Child's Name _____   Week of _____

Sex _____   Birthdate _____

Record of Caregiver/Infant Language Sessions

*Home: M = Mother; F = Father; B = Brother; etc.
Day Care: Teacher 1, 2, 3, etc.

Activity	Mon.	Tues.	Wed.	Thurs.	Fri.	Sat.	Sun.
Toy Play							
Basic Care Routines: 1. Eating 2. Dressing/Changing 3. Washing/Bathing							
Looking at Books and Magazines							
Social Play							
Excursions: 1. Around Home/Day Care 2. Outside Home/Day Care							
Narrating: Happenings, Stories, Discussions, etc.							

* Make a tally mark and the appropriate caregiver code letter for each session involving language stimulation for at least 3 minutes. Place marks opposite the activity and day of the week involved. Enter time estimates in minutes, especially for longer sessions (10 plus minutes), if also desired.

minutes (or tallies) calculated can help you decide where you might want to spend more or less time in language activities. You can even note down the time of day different sessions take place, such as "morning bath," "afternoon snack" or "10:30 AM—6 minutes."

Noting down who conducted each session, as shown in the letter code used in Box 48, can be useful for distributing the amount of time different members of the family or day care staff devote to stimulation.

Checking off each session with a tally mark is obviously easier than stopping to estimate and record the time. Tally marks make a good weekly record of what the family or day care staff is doing from week to week— provided the marks represent something more than just saying a word or sentence or two while changing a diaper or playing with toys. To make a meaningful record each mark needs to reflect at least two or three minutes of play, saying at least a dozen words and sentences in some focused way. You can make an even better account if you also note down any special session that lasts more than several minutes, say 10 or 15 minutes or more. Because they probably won't occur more than two or three times per day, they aren't much trouble to keep a record of.

Ideally, the total number of tally marks per week ranges from about 100 to 120 or so. This means an average of around 15 or more brief sessions per day for each child over the course of each week, counting special language stimulation brought into the various basic care routines of eating, changing-dressing, and washing-bathing as making up half of these, and a couple of sessions each for toy interaction play, looking at picture books, social interaction play and little excursions, either around the house, day care, or on errands. These figures may seem large, but the real issue is whether *language is being consciously incorporated into the basic care and play activities with the baby in a routine way.* One of the purposes of keeping tallies is to help you get in the habit of using language as a matter of course in all interactions with the infant.

Record of the Words Caregivers Use

This is a record of all the words currently being used by the infant's various caregivers in the day-to-day language activities. Most of the recent words used in language play will be recalled if they are written down every week or so, though the record will naturally be more accurate if a list is compiled at the end of each day. Some parents and teachers will want to organize their weekly list of words into columns, following the organization of nouns into categories of activity (e.g., household items,

Box 49

Infant _____

Birthdate _____

Caregiver _____

Period Covered (Dates) _____

Caregiver Word List Form

Common Objects (Nouns)				Common Actions (Verbs)	
Care Routines	Toy Play	Excursions		Actions	Verb-Like Terms
Eating	Replicas	Home/ Day Care	Community	Specific	Expressions
		Indoors	General	Body	
				Hand-Arm	
			Vehicles		Verb-Like Uses of:
				Other	
Dressing			Park/ Playground		
	Other Toys				Adjectives
				General Purpose	
		Yard			Adverbs
			Other Sites		
Washing					

The Actions (Verbs) you label in an activity can be listed either with the Common Actions (Verbs) or with the objects you label (Nouns) for the activity, depending on your preference. Refer to Box 19, Chapter 7 for suggestions of words to use for labeling.

care routines), like those listed in Box 19, Chapter 7. This will help you keep track of what words you are using regularly and what kinds of activity are getting more emphasis than others. Verbs and other parts of speech can be listed in separate columns. It will be remembered that many fewer examples of the more complex parts of speech, such as adjectives and prepositions, and especially adverbs and pronouns, will appear in the early lists of words you use, if the recommended method of introducing the simpler parts of speech first is followed. A simple form for keeping records of words used each week is shown in Box 49.

There is no need to list every word you ever say to the infant, the kind of casual comments people make without really thinking about them, such as "It's about time to finish" or "I forgot to give you your banana this morning." Because the words are not directly linked to the immediate situation and the comments are usually fairly abstract and not repeated, they are usually difficult for infants to understand until they are well along in saying sentences. It doesn't hurt to say them, of course, as long as they don't form the main body of what you say, and you also use lots of concrete nouns and verbs during the sessions. It is useful, however, to list common expressions like "Bye-bye," "Thank you," and "Hi" that the family repeats from time to time.

QUESTIONS ON LANGUAGE STIMULATION THE RECORDS CAN ANSWER

The weekly lists should include all words used fairly frequently from day to day, including both words used for the first time that week and any words that have been used before in prior weeks. In this way, caregivers can get a good idea of just what words and parts of speech they are using with a baby. They may be quite surprised at some of the things they have been saying without realizing it. Are there too many adults giving the baby too many new words each week? The limit should be somewhere around 5 to 15 new ones per week during the early stages of word learning. Are the same few words being used each week, over and over again, so the infant can't expand his or her vocabulary? Are no words included from washing and bathing routines and few outdoor words? Are there too many adjectives and adverbs before the infant can understand them? Are they using too many pronouns, thus confusing the child as to what the label is?

Are they using different labels for the same things? None of these practices are fatal. Infants will certainly learn to talk well and probably at a good pace if they are given a lot of language early, even if it's not perfect. But it does help them to learn when you make a nice balance.

Comparing the Words You Use With the Child's Development

As the child begins to talk, you can compare the words she or he is starting to say with the lists of words you or the day caregivers have been using. If you or the day care staff have been fairly constant in using language in the routines and toy play, and if the lists are fairly accurate, you'll probably find that over half of the child's first 50 words are on the lists of words used. Where did the baby learn the others? In day care there are of course usually several different teachers involved, making it difficult to keep track of everything the different caregivers say. But if parents keep a daily list, perhaps even writing down the words used after each session, and if the child has no experience in day care and little elsewhere with people, they might expect to find their lists match the list of the baby's first 50 words rather closely. In any case, parents and teachers can take a lot of satisfaction from their efforts if they find as many as half a baby's first words on their lists. They must be doing something right.

Things to Do With the Records

What does one do with the long lists likely to accumulate from records of this kind?

Value for Day Care Staff

Teachers find daily records of this kind an invaluable source of feedback on the quality of the language environment in the center, which can be used to modify the program. These cumulative observations inform the staff on not only how well each child is acquiring language at each stage along the way, but also about the quality of the program generally. Because the record of every child is detailed over time, the records furnish information on which children seem to be getting more or less effective attention in language activities, and over what periods of the program.

Depending on their detail, records will also yield information on which aspects of language each child is progressing, for example, among the different parts of speech, the sheer quantity of new words acquired, or the length and complexity of sentences being formed. Thus teachers are able to make changes in the activities and types of language concepts in which each child is engaged according to the developmental patterns and profiles emerging from week to week.

Because of the presence of several teachers in each group, however, it is not always easy to keep exact records for every teacher and know exactly how the language activities are influencing each child's development. Yet staff discussions and records of the frequency and types of language terms employed can furnish many insights to serve as a basis for improving or altering the quality of language each child is experiencing.

Of particular value is scanning records of both teachers and children to identify which children seem to be benefiting least and which most, and in what way, so that staff may shift priorities in specific ways. If, for example, the match between one teacher's list of words she/he uses and the words a certain child is beginning to understand (or say) is high, yet the child is not progressing well, cooperation among teachers may help to bring about changes. Giving the teacher special guidance, switching teacher responsibilities to produce a better match in teacher-child styles, or simply having more teachers devote more time to the child needing more attention to language are among the options available.

The general quality of the program becomes evident in comparing how well the children do on the average, as well as in the percentage of children in the group who are doing well, especially in terms of surpassing norms for language development.

Naturally, not all of the successes and setbacks in various children's development can be attributed to the day care program. The home makes important contributions as well, and may in fact account for a substantial amount of the individual differences appearing between children in their verbal fluency and rates of development. Yet even children with comparatively bland home lives will often thrive in day care and make solid advances in language, given a day care environment rich in language activities. Conversely, language-neglected day care environments may dampen language and other forms of cognitive development, even in children growing up in homes with a high quality of attention to language. After all, children often spend many of their waking hours each week in day care, typically 8 hours a day, five days a week.

Informing and Guiding Parents

Not the least of their functions is the information children's records furnish staff to inform parents in detail about how their child is developing. Often, they can be the basis for suggesting to parents the need to provide more verbal communication and language play in the home. When parents are given a firsthand picture of just how their child is and is not progressing, and in what ways, parents can see for themselves the kind of additional attention the child may need. This information, presented in the context of an understanding discussion between teacher and parent, is likely to furnish parents with both insights and understanding on how to help their child develop. A few suggestions regarding the possibilities of enriching the child's language experiences in the course of the daily basic home care routines alone can go far toward improving the language and relationship climate within the family. Much can be done in this way to avert language delay in the early stages and reassure parents of their children's potentials for development.

Such discussions should by no means be limited to the so-called "problem" or lagging children. Most children have different areas of strength and weakness to review, where changes may help. Some children may be acquiring vocabulary rapidly, but lag in constructing sentences or the quality of syntax, or be developing generally well, but with a narrow range of vocabulary and concepts.

Value for Parents

Daily observations perform much the same functions for the home, whether collected by parents themselves or through the efforts of the child's nanny or caregiver. Some families will want to do no more than look them over from time to time, perhaps sharing them with grandparents and friends or putting them away as mementos of their child's early development.

But many other families will want to use them as guides for changing their language stimulation play in certain ways. The home, moreover, frequently offers certain advantages for tracking an infant's development. If the child is attending a day care program, then parents will of course need to consult with the day care staff to coordinate activities between the home and day care. Typically, the development of only one infant has to be followed, and one parent (or home caregiver), or at most two, are the chief source of the child's language experiences in the home. The problem of getting an accurate picture of the processes and problems of the development of a single child is thus obviously not so complex as following the daily activities of a group of children in day care. For example, if a child shows evidence of understanding what's going on, but seems to make little or no headway in understanding and saying any words, it may mean the actively involved parent is using language that is too complex or spoken too rapidly. The child may be hearing lots of complicated or rapidly spoken sentences, without particular words being connected with particular objects or actions. Thus the child is learning mainly from parent gestures (and his/her own play), which won't give him or her the ability to reason and express ideas in the complex and abstract way that only language makes possible.

Perhaps the child's vocabulary is accumulating rapidly, words pour out of the child, but sentence formation is delayed, because the active caregiver has typically presented words in isolation, out of the context of sentences. Or is the child not saying any adjectives, adverbs, or pronouns, even after piling up 20 or 30 words? Why not? Puzzling over the child's records, comparing them with caregiver records and relating them to caregiver styles can be very helpful in answering these questions.

Graphing the Records

Some parents and teachers may like to assemble these materials to give a long-term picture of language development, compiling sounds, words and sentences in the type of cumulative learning graphs shown earlier (Boxes 41 and 42). Such graphic displays will lend perspective to the child's records. They provide important aids to enrich parent and teacher understanding, serving as feedback for improving the quality of the language environment.

While most parents and many day care programs may not wish to keep detailed long-term records, at least one or two cumulative learning graphs for sounds, words, and perhaps the first few phrases and sentences can be extremely useful for monitoring each child with an eye to checking and improving the quality of language activity. Even short-term records graphing no more than a few weeks of the cumulative learning of, for example, sounds or words, will give a perspective that the recorded lists themselves don't show. They make a useful complement to the information that lists furnish on which words, parts of speech, sentences, and other content details the child is acquiring. They thus add a great deal to picturing just how well a child is progressing.

Research on Early Language Stimulation

The research for the following programs consisted of a series of studies I conducted with students over an extended period of years. Two major studies were conducted in day care settings. Several smaller scale studies were carried out by students with families in home settings, some as seminar projects and others as doctoral dissertations. The day care projects occurred over a period of several years, while the home-based studies provided guidance to parents over periods of 6 months to a year. Follow-up studies of the children's progress were conducted as well.

STUDIES IN DAY CARE

Research in a Private Agency

My first study in which language occupied a central place was a three year longitudinal project on day care for infants from a few weeks to 18 months of age (Fowler, 1972). I was asked by a private agency in Toronto, Canada to collaborate in designing, developing, and evaluating a high quality day care program. Known as Canadian Mothercraft Society, the organization had long been devoted to training young working class women to serve as nannies for middle and upper income families. This new program would also serve as a training program for day care teachers.

This program provided an ideal day care environment, set in an elegant Victorian mansion with many well-lighted and well-equipped rooms, a large number of toys and learning materials, and exceptional teacher-child ratios. The size of the teacher training program often made possible a single teacher for every one or two children. The result was a highly enriched program that allowed a great deal of closely supervised free play, relaxed and stimulating care in the basic child care routines of dressing, washing, eating, and napping; it also included a variety of special play and learning activities. The centerpiece of the activities was sensitive, interactive care with the babies accompanied by focused language stimulation. Teachers were shown how to talk to the babies using the routines we describe in this book. Interactive language play was a fundamental exercise for children of all ages. The program in day care was coordinated with a program for parents that included periodic home visits and phone communication by a parent guidance worker in methods of improving basic care and enriching language and other cognitive activities. There was also a circulating toy library for less educated, poorer families in the project.

Results

The results of this project surprised us all, given the fact that while most of the parents were of middle class educated backgrounds, they were often either single parent or two working parent families. Over the three-year period, the research staff found that children gained an average of 19 IQ points on the Bayley Scales (Bayley, 1969), reaching a mean IQ of 130. The first-year sample, which embraced a broader age span that had attended for a shorter period than later cohorts, reached a mean IQ of 127, significantly more than the 110 IQ for the home-reared comparison group (the only controls for this project). The small sample of infants from families with less education gained an average of 16 points to reach a mean IQ of 116, much higher than culturally expected norms for these infants. On measures of social and emotional development, children developed similarly well compared to controls in such characteristics as enthusiasm, gregariousness, and verbal expressiveness.

But the most interesting finding was the outstanding gains children made in language development; they significantly exceeded the development of the comparison group of home-reared children in vocabulary, social communication, and active expression as well as in comprehension. Even before seeing the results of the formal measures, it was evident to everyone, staff and visitors alike, how verbal the program babies became over the course of their time in the enrichment program.

Research in A Municipal Center

My second major research project in which language stimulation from infancy occupied a central place consisted of a five-year project in the first municipally run infant day care center in Canada (Fowler, 1978). This project was also by invitation, in this case by the Department of Social Services of Metropolitan Toronto. The study was funded jointly by the Canada Department of National Health and Welfare and the Research Planning Branch of the Ontario Ministry of Community and Social Services.

We employed much the same methods in this study and the day care staff was trained in much the same way by our research staff. There were, however, no students in training. The day care teachers had some minimum training in medically oriented European facilities, but did not have a great deal of background in child development or early education. Home care was enriched and coordinated with the day care program, as in the first project, but the toy library circulated to all families in this project. The day care environment, while not as spacious and elegant as the Victorian mansion, consisted of a nicely remodeled old house.

Infants entered the program at slightly older ages, beginning after 6 months instead of as early as 6 weeks as in the first study. The teacher-child ratios were also generally slightly lower, averaging 2.5 infants per teacher for children between 6 and 18 months, and 5.6 infants per teacher for the toddlers up to 30 months. The infants all came from single parent families (by agency policy); parents had a high school education or less, and were from a variety of ethnic backgrounds. The matched comparison group, however, were all two-parent families.

The program was essentially the same as in the first study, except that there was not as much individual attention available to the children. To ensure that no child "got lost in the shuffle" in these circumstances, we introduced a monitoring system. Teachers were asked to see that every infant was engaged in interactive language toy play several times each day, tallying each session and the time under the child's name on a wall chart that was changed weekly. On the average, each child enjoyed 2 to 3 sessions per day.

Development During the Infant Program

Our findings in this study were again similar to those in the three-year study, but with certain important differences. In this study, we used the Griffiths Mental Development Scales (Griffiths, 1954; 1970) that gave us measures of ability in several areas of competence (language, spatial problem solving, personal-social, fine and gross motor, and math concepts) that provided a profile of how each child developed. These scales furnished a more reliable measure of language development than the measures used in the previous day care study. Over the course of the five-year study, we found that stimulated infants consistently gained a few IQ points in all abilities between program entry and 30 to 36 months of age, compared to the home-reared children, who remained the same or declined slightly. But the average gains were most outstanding in language and spatial problem solving, ranging between 15 and 25 IQ points, reaching means of 120 to 125 IQ on the two scales. Other measures of children's socioemotional development and motivations, made through observations during play, again showed highly positive development.

Development During the Preschool Program

When we continued to follow these same students as they entered the preschool program (ages 3-5) in the same day care center, we saw the reverse finding, a decline in scores. Also, the difference between the day care and home-reared children disappeared. The day care children tended to fall back toward average levels of functioning, while the home-reared children tended to progress better in all measures. We accounted for this finding by examining the preschool day care program.

The teacher-child ratios in the older age groups were much higher (1 teacher to 9 children) than in the infant and toddler groups. While this does not directly suggest that the children experienced poor care, it does mean that these teachers had no time to participate in the inservice training sessions with the research staff and had not learned the enrichment methods the infant/toddler teachers were trained in. Because of this, they could not maintain the enriched, individualized program.

On the other hand, the home-reared children, who all came from two-parent families, stimulated their children more during this preschool period. What became clear was that these parents did not expect much from their infants until they reached the preschool years. Even then they did not enrich their preschoolers with the intensity of our day care program during infancy. They still needed to be convinced that frequent interactive contacts were beneficial to their child's continuing development. But their stimulation and interactions seemed to increase the average scores for the home-reared children, although they never attained the levels for language and other skills reached by the day care children during infancy.

From these findings, two points are worth stressing. On the one hand, it is evident that the effects of the early enrichment generally declined when the enrichment was not sustained into the preschool period. All children, both day care and home reared, developed from then on at only slightly above average levels. On the other hand, the effects of enrichment during infancy were sustained best in language development with day care children generally maintaining above average levels even while attending the less enriched preschool day care program.

STUDIES IN THE HOME

Because of these positive findings, I decided to work with parents in the home (Fowler, 1983, 1990), concentrating on guiding them in enriching their child's language environment, the area that seemed to influence development most in the day care studies. Among the chief purposes of these studies was to determine just how vital language was to development, how fluent children could become as a result of furnishing highly enriched language experiences from infancy on.

In these home care studies, parents were responsible for their child's general care. Our research group furnished guidance for language enrichment beyond what the individual parents would normally do in following the practices of their own cultural and educational background.

Working with students on doctoral dissertations, students in seminars, and through several case studies, I conducted a series of studies embracing a total of 48 infants plus various controls. In these studies, we generally began guiding the parents when the infant ranged between 3 and 7 months of age, using essentially the same methods developed in the day care settings. Most of the families were two-parent families, with the mother caring for her first-born child at home herself during infancy. These circumstances maximized parent motivations and opportunities to enrich the child's environment. The families came from a broad spectrum of educational backgrounds and ethnic groups, including some Italian-speaking families who were functionally illiterate and a Chinese-speaking group.

An additional study by Gloria Roberts (Fowler, 1983) of 21 Afro-Caribbean infants from low income families with a high school education or less involved a one-year general cognitive learning program which included much language stimulation, 11 infants starting around 3.5 months and 10 at 13.5 months. These provided a good test of how important language is to children's development. Because we used the same multi-competence scales used in the second day care study, we also obtained information on how early language enrichment influenced development in other areas of mental development.

Infant Development in the Home Care Studies

What we found is that all infants, without exception, gained in all areas of ability measured, but especially in language competence, well beyond the levels normally expected from the children's cultural and educational backgrounds. In all cases children advanced substantially more than norms and in general significantly more than children in the various control and comparison groups. Children from both the Italian and Chinese-speaking families averaged mean language IQ's around 125 to 135 by the age of 12 months, while the bulk of the children, all from educated, English-speaking families, typically attained language quotients of at least 140 by the ages of 12 to 24 months or more.

The study with low income, low education Afro-Caribbean infants found the infants attaining language quotients of 124 and 121 for the respective younger and older starting groups, as well as making generally strong cognitive gains in other areas that reflected the general cognitive sweep of the program. Interestingly, in one of the language stimulation studies, children in a comparison group of infants who were furnished special activities in baby gymnastics, also advanced remarkably in language skills. How could this be? These unexpected advances were found to be brought about by parents using language extensively in the exercise games.

Children in all of the home care studies tended to gain in general abilities such as social competence and in problem solving and reasoning skills, though not to quite the same levels of advantage as in language. Gains were more consistent in the children from more advantaged educational backgrounds, but there were no consistent gender differences.

Most interesting were the consistent signs of rich verbal competence and fluency in all the children. On the average, infants said their first real words by 8 months, at least 5 words by 9 months, between 10 and 20 words by 10 months and 50 or more words by 15 months, much ahead of the usual developmental norms (See Box 2, Chapter 2). Their first two-word combinations typically appeared by one year, 3-word sentences by 15 months, and lengthy sentences by 18 months, compared to the usual age of 3 years (36 months).

These are not just narrow measures of acceleration. The best evidence of the richness of their mastery of language is reflected in the early ability of the children to participate in extended conversations and talk meaningfully about their experiences, following clear and coherent themes (see Stage IV activities in Chapter 9). Many of these babies could do this by 18 months; quite a number of them learned slightly earlier. Language was thus becoming a useful tool for communicating and getting along. Many parents commented on how much easier it was to cope with their children, compared with other infants they observed. They could readily follow instructions, grasp the family social rules, and understand things quickly. It was more stimulating to be around them and play with them, because they responded enthusiastically and learned so easily.

Later Development

In the day care studies, we have limited follow-up information on children in the private agency study and none in the municipal day care center study. Three follow-up studies were conducted in the private agency study, at the respective mean ages of 47 and 55 months, and at just over 9 years. At the first follow up, mean language and general IQ scores were 130 and 120 respectively; at the second, mean IQ scores were 134 on the Binet. No separate language scores were available.

At the second follow-up study (unpublished), data are available on seven children who had participated extensively in the original language enrichment program (14 to 22 months). The verbal IQ's (WISC) of five children whose parents had maintained a rich home environment were 124, which is moderately high for the WISC (Weschler,1949). Their full scale was 119. The verbal IQ's of two children whose later home environments were less stimulating fell to average levels (101 and 96). Further follow-up studies of all day care children are being planned.

Nearly all home reared children continued to maintain high verbal fluency and cognitive skills during early follow-up studies from ages 2 1/2 to 3 1/2. Although a few children declined slightly, usually in association with heightened family problems, most lags among children from both high school and college educated families were temporary and no child failed to maintain levels above cultural norms.

Follow-up studies during later development in high school and college have yielded the most interesting findings on the effects of early language enrichment (Fowler, Ogston, Roberts-Fiati, and Swenson (1993, 1994, 1995). Of 40 students (of the original 44) from families with at least one year of college, 68% have attained gifted status, 80 to 93% have excellent verbal competencies (ranging from creative writing skills to mastering one or more foreign languages), 70% are highly skilled in math, 75% in science, 78% in one or more art form (music, drama, visual arts, dance), 75% in sports, and 85% socially. Moreover, 93% are independently motivated intellectually and 63% are intellectual leaders.

Among 16 students from families with only 4 to 12 years of education (both parents), including Afro-Caribbean immigrant families, 63% have excelled in school, 31% have been in gifted programs, 38 to 81% have excellent reading, writing and foreign language learning skills, 31% excel in math, 38% in science, 69% in one or more art form, 44% in sports, and 88% socially. Among these students, 81% are intellectually independently motivated and 31% are intellectual leaders. Among the 10 controls of the Afro-Caribbean students, who did not experience the early language enrichment research program, only 10% have done well in school and none are gifted.

We are continuing to study the later development of our early language enriched students, including how and in what way families, schools and the community appear to support and build on the competencies of enriched children. It is however already evident that an important element of the children's early competencies is found in the exceptional motivations the combined socially-cognitively oriented language enrichment provides. The later success of these children appears to result in large part from the high interest and marked self-directedness of the children. These early established characteristics have made them initiate a great deal of their later learning on their own, as well as to respond to the enhanced opportunities and stimulation from others that their exceptional skills attract.

References

Bayley, N. (1969). *Bayley scales of infant development.* New York, NY. The Psychological Corporation.

Brigance, A.H. (1978). *Diagnostic Inventory of Early Development.* North Billerica, MA: Curriculum Associates.

Brown, R. (1973). *A first language.* Cambridge, MA: MIT Press.

Bzoch, K.R., & League, R. (1971). *Assessing language skills in infancy.* Austin, TX: Pro-Ed.

Carew, J. (1980). Experience and the development of intelligence in young children at home and in day care. *Monographs of the Society for Research in Child Development, 45,* Serial No. 187.

Clarke-Stewart, K.A. (1973). Interactions between mothers and their young children: Characteristics and consequences. *Monographs of the Society for Research in Child Development, 38,* Serial No. 153.

Consortium for Longitudinal Studies. (1983). *As the twig is bent: Lasting effects of preschool programs.* Hillsdale, NJ: Lawrence Erlbaum.

Dunn, L.M. (1965). *Peabody picture vocabulary test.* Minneapolis, MN: American Guidance Service.

Fenson, L., Dale, P.S., Reznick, J.S., Thal, D., Bates, E., Hartung, J.P., Pethick, S., and Reilly, J.S. (1993). *MacArthur Communicative Development Inventories.* San Diego: Singular Publishing Group.

Fowler, W. (1972). A developmental learning approach to infant care in a group setting. *Merrill-Palmer Quarterly, 18,* 145-175.

Fowler, W. (1978). *Day care and its effects on early development: A study of group and home care in multi-ethnic, working-class families.* Toronto, Canada: Ontario Institute for Studies in Education.

Fowler, W. (1983). *Potentials of childhood; Volumes 1 &2,* Lexington, MA: Lexington Books.

Fowler, W. (1990). Early stimulation and the development of verbal talents. In M.J.A. Howe (ed.), *Encouraging the development of exceptional abilities and talents.* London, UK: British Psychological Society.

Fowler, W., Ogston, K., Roberts-Fiati, G., and Swenson, A. (1993). Accelerating Language Acquisition. In K. K. Ackrill (ed.) *The Origins and Development of High Ability.* Chichester, UK: Wiley.

Fowler, W., Ogston, K., Roberts-Fiati, G., and Swenson, A. (1994). Long-term Effects in high school after enrichment in infancy. Poster presented at the Ninth International Conference on Infant Studies. Paris, June 2–5.

Fowler, W., Ogston, K., Roberts-Fiati, G., and Swenson, A. (1995). Early enrichment and later giftedness and competencies in children from different backgrounds. Poster presented at the Biennial Meeting of the Society for Research in Child Development, Indianapolis, Indiana. March 30–April 2, 1995.

Fowler, W. & Swenson, A. (1979). The influence of early language stimulation on development. *Genetic Psychology Monographs, 100,* 73-109.

Garber, H.L. & Heber, R. (1981). The efficacy of early intervention with family rehabilitation. In M.J. Begab, H.C. Haywood, and H.L. Garber (eds.), *Volume 2: Psychosocial influences in retarded performance; Strategies for improving competence.* Baltimore, MD: University Park Press.

Griffiths, R. (1954). *The abilities of babies.* London, UK: University of London Press.

Griffiths, R. (1970). *The abilities of young children.* London, UK: University of London Press.

Grogan, W.R. (1990). Engineering's silent crisis. *Science, 247,* 381.

Hedrick, D.L., Prather, E.M., & Tobin, A.R. (1975). *Sequenced inventory of communication development (SICD).* Seattle, WA: University of Washington Press.

Hunt, J. McV. (1986). The effect of variations in quality and type of early child care on development. In W. Fowler (ed.), *Early experience and the development of competence.* Volume 32; *New Directions for Child Development.* San Francisco, CA: Jossey-Bass.

Huttenlocher, J., Height, W., Bryk, A., Seltzer, M., and Lyons, T. (1991). Early vocabulary growth: Relation to language input and gender. *Developmental Psychology, 27,* 236–248.

Lee, L.L. (1974). *Developmental sentence analysis: A grammatical assessment procedure for speech and language clinicians.* Evanston, IL: Northwestern University Press.

McCartney, K. (1984). Effect of quality of day care environment on children's language development. *Developmental Psychology, 20,* 244-260.

Menyuk, P. (1977). *Language and maturation.* Cambridge, MA: MIT Press.

Miller, J., & Chapman, R. (1981). The relation between age and mean length of utterance in morphemes. *Journal of Speech and Hearing Research, 24,* 154-161.

Miller, J.F. and Paul, R. (1994). *The Clinical Assessment of Language Comprehension.* Baltimore: Brookes.

Nelson, K. (1973). Structure and strategy in learning to talk. *Monographs of the Society for Research in Child Development, 38,* Serial No. 149.

Rosch, E.R. (1973). Natural categories. *Cognitive Psychology, 4,* 328-350.

Snow, C.E., & Ferguson, C.A. (Eds.). (1977). *Talking to children.* Cambridge, UK: Cambridge University Press.

Vigotsky, L.S. (1962). *Thought and language.* Cambridge, MA: MIT Press.

Weir, R.H. (1962). *Language in the crib.* The Hague: Mouton.

Wechsler, David. (1949). *Wechsler intelligence scale for children.* New York, NY: The Psychological Corporation.

Zigler, E. & Valentine, J. (Eds.). (1979). *Project head start: A legacy of the war on poverty.* New York, NY: The Free Press.

Author's Biography

Dr. William Fowler, M.A. Harvard, Ph.D. University of Chicago. Director, Center for Early Learning and Child Care, Cambridge, Massachusetts.

William Fowler is a clinical and developmental psychologist. He is the author of many research articles and several books on early education and child care. Among his other books are a two volume textbook on *Infant and Child Care* and a two volume work on *Potentials of Childhood*. He has conducted extensive research on infant and child development and learning in home and school settings, designed and evaluated infant day care programs and was principal of the University of Chicago Laboratory Nursery School. He has taught at Yale, Harvard, the University of Chicago, more recently at Tufts University, and was for many years a Professor of Applied Psychology at the Ontario Institute for Studies in Education, University of Toronto.

Index

---

advanced sound play activities, 110
  nonsense word play, 111
    increases sensitivity to sound
      patterns, 112
    strategies for, 113
  play with meaning, 111
  poetry and song in play, 111

baby talk, 84
Bayley, N., 220
behavioral strategies, 166
  disadvantages of, 166
  for correcting language delay, 167
  vs. cognitive learning, 167
Brown, R., 194

Carew, J., 8
Clarke-Stewart, K.A., 8
classics, 126
  Beatrix Potter series, 126
  Blueberries for Sal, 126
  Good Night Moon, 126
cognitive developmental stimulation, 165
cognitive strategies, 168
  advantages of, 168
communication, verbal modes, 162
  shifting from gestural to verbal, 163
  spontaneous speech, 165
competence goals, vi
  in modern world, vi
comprehension, testing of, 107
Consortium for Longitudinal Studies, x
correcting language errors at different
  stages, 174, 176
  Stage I:
    first sounds, 199
    pronunciation, 176, 199

Stages II & III:
  first phrases and sentences, 206
  first words, 202
  using language play, 177
  words and sentences, 110, 177,
    193
Stage IV:
  first steps, 179
  problems with theme learning,
    23, 57, 178, 209, 225
  sociodramatic play, 180
  theme development, 180

Developmental Sentence Analysis (DSA),
  196
Developmental Sentence Scoring (DSS),
  196
Developmental Sentence Types (DST),
  196
Dunn, L.M., 192

expectations of book, x
  how to use, xii
experience, importance of, 2
  adult speech, 2

Fowler, W., x, 8, 121, 192, 219, 221, 223,
  226
Fowler, W., & Swenson, A., 190

Garber, H.L., & Heber, R., x
Griffiths Mental Development Scales, 10,
  221
Griffiths, R., 221
Grogan W.R., vi

hearing loss, 169

informal & professional evaluations, 170-172
Hedrick, D.L., Prather, E.M., & Tobin, A.R., 192
Hunt, J. McV., x

interaction activities, 35
  excursions, 59
    at day care, 63
    at home, inside, 60
    at home, outside, 62
    community, 65
    neighborhood, 64
  excursions, problems of, 66
    backpacks, 67, 68
    carriages & slings, 68, 69
    car seats, 68
  home-made picture books, 51
  places to play, 40
  playing with toys, 35
    play setting, 35
    toy storage, 38
  social activity play, 57
    verse and song, 57, 58
  television, 54

labeling relationships, 90
  parts of speech, 92
    simple, 92
    complex, 92
  simple to complex speech, 90
  language, vii
    central role, 3
    early development, 10
    early stimulation, vii
    importance of, vii
    nature of, 4
language achievements, daily records, 198
  evidence of understanding, 204
  increasing use of private speech, 206
  recording circumstances, 205
  what to record, 200
language delay, 155
  catching up, 158
  correction of, 155
  developmental profile, 172
    diagnosing, 169
    gestures, 160
    meaning of, 155
    speech lag, 155
    temporary, 156
      benchmarks of, 162
      degrees of, 161
language development, 7
  course of, 7
  later stages, 11
  order & experience, 8
  successive stages, 18-19
language enrichment, iv
  effect on development, 9
language learning, 186
  audio- and videotaping, 193
    planning & preparation, 194
  cyclical course, 188
  different rates of, 189
  gradual learning, 187
  rules, 186
  synthesis: understanding rules, 187
language stimulation, stages, 15, 16, 18, 42
  adapting to child's understanding, 28
  cognitive strategy, 27
  during basic care routines, 42
    dressing/undressing, 43
    eating, 47
    naps & bedtime, 49
    talking, 46
    washing/bathing, 45
  labeling, timing & precision, 26
  over- and under-directing, 25
  play
    construction, 33
    sociodramatic, 31
  principles of, 23-25
    interaction, 24
  relating to infant, 25
  sentences, sound patterns, word combinations, 16
  starting late, 17
Lee, L.L., 196

McCartney, K., 64
Mean Length of Utterance (MLU), 194

Menyuk, p., 10
Miller, J., & Chapman, R., 195
Mother Goose Nursery Rhymes, 153

narrating experiences, 130, 131
    arousing interest, 133
    conversations, 135
        guiding, 136
        large families & day care groups,
            138
    developing narrative skills, 132
    discussions, 139
    early steps, 131
    in small groups, 134
    mealtimes, importance of, 137
    participation, 138
    sociodramatic play, 140
        dramatic skits, organizing, 143
        guiding, 141
        importance of language in, 141
        parent guide to, 144, 145
        role play, occupational, 142
        social play time, 146
Nelson, K., 81
New Haven Parent Early Education, iii

pacifiers, 94
    excessive vs. judicious use, 94, 95
    use at day care, 95
    use at home, 96
parts of speech, 81
    nouns, 81
    plurals, tenses, pronouns, 86-89
    prepositions, 82
    verbs, 82
    word curriculum, suggestions for, 83
parts of speech, roles of, 103
    phrase & clause manipulation, 106
        flexibility & simplicity, 106
    word substitution play, 105
Peabody Picture Vocabulary Test, 192
phrases and sentences in play, 101
    expansion and substitution play, 108
    sentence play, 101
    mastering complex parts of speech in
        early stages, 102
    speech play, functional roles, 104

poetry and singing, 151
    appreciation of, 152
    music, 151
    reading poetry, 153
    social play with verse, 152
progress of infants, what to measure, 183
    daily observation, 184
        unobtrusive, 208
    formal testing, 184, 185
    graphing records, 217
    professional measures, 192
    Type/Token Ratio, 195
    record keeping, 210-214
        value for day care staff, 214
        value for parents, 216
pronouns, activities for learning, 109

reading to children, 121
    introducing topics, 127
    poetry, 126
    science & nonfiction, 126
    stories, 121
        arousing interest, 125
        early steps, 121
        gender roles & ethnic groups,
            124
        listening to, 123
        moving from objects to scenes,
            122
        reading text, 124
rearing children, v
    contemporary society, v
    early times, v
Receptive-Expressive Emergent
    Language Scale (REEL), 10, 192
research on early language stimulation,
    219
    development,221
        during infant program, 221
        during preschool program, 222
    studies at day care, 219
        in private agency, 219
            results, 220
        in municipal center, 220
    studies at home, 223
        infants, 224
        later development, 225

Rosch, E.R., 28

Sequenced Inventory of Communicative Development (SICD), 192
Snow, C.E., & Ferguson, C. A., 86
Stage I: Vocalization Play, 71
    adding new sounds, 72
    emotional benefits, 72
    establishing dialogue, 72
        steps to dialogue, 73
    variations, talking with infants, 74
    word labeling, 79
Stage II: Playing with Words, Labeling, 77, 78
    advantages, 77, 79
    how it works, 78
Stage III: Playing with Phrases & Sentences, 101
    early stages, 104
    functional roles of speech play, 104
    learning roles of parts of speech, 103
    mastering complex parts of speech, 102
    nonsense words, 11, 113
    testing comprehension, 107
    whole phrases & clauses, 106

word substitution play, 105
Stage IV: Theme Activities, 119
    reading & narrating, 119
    value of theme experience, 120
stimulating sound development, 97
    verse & song, 97
stimulation of infants in learning, 114
    enrichment discontinued,
    results of, 115 social rewards, 115
storytelling, 147
    developing skills, 150
    encouraging skills, 148
    two avenues to, 149

theme development, 197
    complexity, 197
    variety, 197

Vygostsky, L.S., 206

Wechsler, D., 225
Wechsler Intelligence Scale for Children (WISC), 225
Weir, R.H., 208

Zigler, E., & Valentine, J., x